7.95

A-10

WARTHOG

D & S
Vol. 19
Close Air Support
Tank Killer!

 in detail & scale

Dana Bell

D1616645

AERO
A division of TAB BOOKS Inc.
Blue Ridge Summit, PA 17214

This book is a product of Detail & Scale, Inc., which has sole responsibility for its content and layout, except that all contributors are responsible for the security clearance and copyright release of all materials submitted. Published and distributed in the United States by TAB BOOKS, Inc., and in London and Melbourne by Arms and Armour Press.

CONTRIBUTORS:

R. J. Archer
Lt. Col. Buddy Beall (MDANG)
Capt. John E. Charlton (422nd TES)
Bob DeMayo
Robert Duff (AFSC/PAG)
Jim Galloway
Lt. Col. Francis C. Guideon, Jr. (AFSC)
Jim Hogey
Bert Kinzey
Al Lloyd
Greg L. Marshall
David W. Menard
Kirk Minert
Sgt. Frank Nauman
Doug Remington

Theron Rinehart (Fairchild Republic)
Brian C. Rogers
Mick Roth
John P. Santucci
Lt. Col. Eric Solander (USAF Mag & Books Branch)
Robert C. Stern
George Thune (Fairchild Republic)
Sgt. Dave Turnbull (MDANG)
USAF
Amn. Tracy White (MDANG)
Larry Wilson
Wally Van Winkle
Maj. Les Wood (HQUSAF)
Bob Young

Most photos in this book are credited to their contributors. Photos with no credit indicated were taken by the author.

DEDICATION
"For Susie"

FIRST EDITION
FIRST PRINTING

Printed in the United States by

TAB BOOKS Inc.
P.O. Box 40
Blue Ridge Summit, PA 17214

Library of Congress Cataloging
in Publication Data

Bell, Dana
A-10 Warthog (the tank killer).

(Detail and Scale ; vol. 19)
  1. A-10 (Jet attack plane)
  I. Title.
  UG1242.A28B45   1986
  623.74'63
  85-31757
  ISBN 0-8168-5030-5 (pbk.)

British Library Cataloging in
Publication Data

Bell, Dana
A-10 Warthog: the tank killer.
(Detail & scale series; 19)
  1. A - 10 (Jet attack plane)
  I. Title   II. Series
  623.74'64   UG1242.A28

  ISBN 0-85368-654-8

Front cover: An A-10A from the 357th TFTS, 355th TTW, makes a low-level firing pass for the camera.   (USAF)

Rear cover: Main instrument panel in an A-10A.   (Kinzey)

Airframe 82-665, the 713th and last A-10A to be produced, rolls down the ramp at the Hagerstown production facility.
(Fairchild Republic)

INTRODUCTION

It is curious that most of us still regard the A-10 as a new and exciting aircraft. The last A-10 left the Fairchild production lines in March of 1984, twelve years after the first YA-10 rolled out in 1972. In those twelve years, 715 A-10's were built, and, with the exception of the two prototypes and one tandem-seat modification, the basic airframe design has remained unchanged: simple and unsophisticated.

So far, the operational years of the A-10 have been relatively peaceful; even though a handful of Warthogs were deployed to the Caribbean during 1983's invasion of Granada, none saw action over the island. Yet a baptism of fire might have had one minor advantage: it could have ended a debate that has hounded the Hog since its earliest day. The Press, military, Congress, and the public will probably continue to argue whether such a slow, uncomplicated aircraft can survive ground attack missions in the high threat arena.

Although many in the U.S. Air Force express faith in the concept and the aircraft, that faith has not been echoed by overseas orders - the USAF has been Fairchild Republic's only customer! Partly, this can be attributed to economic considerations, with few nations willing to invest in an aircraft dedicated solely to eliminating ground threats. Many would prefer attaching the mission to an existing high speed fighter, or an attack helicopter, or even a high altitude bomber. Britain's new Tornado for example, can attack ground targets and still fly to altitude and mix it up with Floggers and Fishbeds.

But when it comes to standing and slugging it out with ground forces, the A-10 is still the best aircraft to do the job. Although its top speed is slow, most strike aircraft would have to limit themselves to the same regime to be certain of hitting their targets. No other aircraft can carry as much ordnance over a target for so long, doling out and taking as much punishment, returning to an unimproved field to quickly turn around and strike at an enemy again.

So the A-10 stands ready to perform the mission for which it was designed, the world's premier ground attack aircraft.

HOG FLIGHT

Oh, I have slipped the safe bonds of Earth

And lurched the sky on greasy, wobbling wings.

Cloudward I've lumbered and joined the tumbling mirth

Of instrument flight and done a hundred things

You have not dreamed of · slipped and skidded and swung

High in the bombing pattern. Stalling there

I've chased the elusive pipper along and flung

My body down to drop the bomb I know not where.

Up, up the deliriously high pop I flew

And topped the windswept heights with no airspeed

Which neither Phantom nor even Eagle will ever do.

And while, with rudder and stick atwirl, I pivot

To check six, should I not watch my steed,

I'll dip down my wing . . . and take a divot.

With permission of Captain Dale Hill

(with sincerest apologies to John Gillespie Magee Jr)

ARTWORK © HANK CARUSO 1982

THE PROTOTYPES

Vietnam War air attacks against heavily defended ground targets taught the USAF much about its need for a specialized close air support (CAS) aircraft. In 1967, with the LTV A-7D Corsair II entering production, the Air Force approached the industry for an aircraft which would be cheaper and slower than the A-7D, but more capable than the prop-driven Douglas A-1 Skyraider. In May 1970 a request for proposals (RFP) was issued along more refined requirements signaling the beginning of what would become the 'A-X' (Attack-Experimental) aircraft program. The winner of this 'fly-before-buy' competition was expected to be responsive without regard to weather and to mesh with existing Air Force and Army systems. It would have to be lethal, carrying heavy payloads and massive firepower. It would have to be able to survive in high threat areas, being less vulnerable to enemy ground fire than existing aircraft, and still be uncomplicated, needing minimal maintenance hours per flight hour.

In December 1970, Northrop and Fairchild Republic were each contracted to build two prototypes, which were designated the YA-9 and YA-10, respectively.

Fairchild's simple design placed two turbofan engines on either side of the fuselage, above and behind the wing.

The engines were thus less vulnerable to foreign object damage on rough fields; they could also be left running while ground crews safely reloaded and refueled the aircraft. Mounting the engines on opposite sides of the fuselage reduced the probability that damage to one engine would effect the other, and allowed the fuselage and wings to help mask both power plants from ground fire.

The YA-10s would be powered by the same General Electric TF34-2 turbofans used in the Lockheed S-3A Viking. The TF34s had a higher thrust than the Lycoming F102s used by the YA-9s, and a higher price to match. The General Electric Company became an Air Force co-contractor (as opposed to a Fairchild subcontractor), for the development of a TF34-100 version of the engine of improved compatibility with the A-10A airframe.

The wings were mounted low on the fuselage for easy loading of up to eleven pylons. The main landing gear was placed in sponsons ahead of the main spar, with a wide track to improve rough field handling.

Additional Air Force contracts were let for the design and production of a new anti-armor 30mm cannon that could be mounted in either A-X design. This weapon alone would give the A-X a major offensive advantage over any other ground attack aircraft. Until the new gun, to be known as the GAU-8, could be developed, all four A-X prototypes flew with M61 20mm Gatling guns.

The first YA-10 made its initial test flight at Edwards AFB, California, on 10 May 1972. With the second prototype, (which first flew on 21 July) it was flight-tested until mid-October. From then through the end of the year, differences between the competitors were identified and magnified in a series of difficult flying profiles. In January 1973, the Air Force announced the selection of the A-10 as winner of the A-X competition. Evaluators had found no significant difference in weapons delivery accuracy between the competitors, but the A-10 exhibited superior ground handling qualities and had easier hardpoint access under a wing which had room for more ordnance. The A-10 was closer to production, with a simpler design which appeared likely to keep the flyaway cost closer to the then-estimated $1.4 million per unit. Most evaluation pilots preferred the A-10 for combat operations. The Office of the Secretary of Defense approved full-scale development of the A-10A on 18 January 1972. On the first of March, Fairchild was awarded a contract to continue prototype testing and build ten preproduction aircraft.

Problems with a skeptical Congress surfaced soon after the A-10's selection. As early as 1972, Congress had raised legitimate questions about the need for any new Air Force CAS aircraft while the A-7D was available and the Army was planning advanced armed attack helicopters. The A-10's high production cost and apparent lack of versatility, added to questions about its chances for survival over European battlefields, brought recommendations for an A-7D/A-10 flyoff. The contest was opposed by both the Secretaries of Defense and the Air Force, who protested that the comparison would provide no meaningful new information about combat vulnerability, or rough field operations. Air Force studies had already shown that the A-10 held distinct advantages over the A-7D or any other aircraft suitable for close air support. Congress held to its "recommendation" that experienced combat pilots evaluate and compare both

aircraft. And as a reminder of who controlled the purse strings, in July 1973, the Senate Armed Services Committee cut the number of preproduction airframes from ten to six.

The military acquiesced, and in spring 1974, an A-7D and the second prototype YA-10 met at McConnell AFB, Kansas, to make simulated attacks on Army targets at nearby Fort Riley. The prototype had not yet had a 30mm gun installed, nor were its head-up display (HUD), Maverick launch system, or countermeasures equipment installed. Backed by a team of TAC and AF Systems Command ground observers, four Air Force pilots with close-air combat time flew both test aircraft. The aircrews came from F-100s or F-4s, with none having A-7 or A-10 experience. In one test, with both aircraft carrying eighteen 500 pound bombs on a 260 nautical mile mission, the A-10 remained on station for two hours compared to the A-7's eleven minutes. As expected, the A-10 was found to have greater lethality, a better chance of surviving (due to its hardness), and to be a less expensive aircraft to fly. The report was delivered to Congress in June.

In February 1974, the GAU-8 gun was mounted in the first prototype, firing combat ammunition in June. Gun gas disturbances of the engine were defrayed by a double baffled deflector, and a flame suppressant was added to the round propellant. In July the GAU-8 was declared compatible with the A-10.

TF34-GE-100 engine qualification was completed in October, marking the last milestone prior to completion of the preproduction airframes.

On April 15th, 1975, the first prototype was retired after 467 flights and 590.9 flight hours. The airframe was shipped to Griffiss AFB, New York, where it served on as a ground-based target for electronic countermeasures development. Prototype #2 was placed in flyable storage on 13 June 1975. Shortly afterward, it was transferred to the Air Force Orientation Group (AFOG), fitted with a damaged GAU-8 taken from an A-10 wreck, and sent around the country as part of a traveling static display. The plane is now on exhibit at the Air Force Museum at Wright-Patterson AFB, Ohio.

The first prototype on its maiden test flight over Edwards AFB on 10 May 1972. White lateral stripes help gauge the flap position, which (like the landing gear) was fixed for the entire flight. (USAF)

YA-10 and A-10A SERIAL NUMBERS
(and production sequence numbers)

YA-10s	71-1369	and 71-1370	(prototypes)
A-10As	73-1664 (1)	thru 73-1669 (6)	(preproduction)
	75-258 (7)	thru 75-309 (58)	
	76-512 (59)	thru 76-554 (101)	
	77-177 (102)	thru 77-276 (201)	
	78-582 (202)	thru 78-725 (345)	
	79-082 (346)	thru 79-225 (489)	
	80-140 (490)	thru 80-283 (633)	
	81-939 (634)	thru 81-998 (693)	
	82-646 (694)	thru 82-665 (713)	

A-10 UNIT CODES, UNITS, AND LOCATIONS

AD	Armament Division (AFSC)	Eglin AFB, FL
AK	18 TFS (AAC)	Eielson AFB, AK
BD	917 TFG (AFRES)	Barksdale AFB, LA
CT	103 TFG (ANG)	Connecticut Air Guard
DM	355 TTW (TAC)	Davis-Monthan AFB, AZ
ED*	AFFTC (AFSC)	Edwards AFB, CA
EL	23 TFW (TAC)	England AFB, LA
IN	45 TFS (AFRES)	Grissom AFB, IN
KC	442 TFW (AFRES)	Richards-Gebaur AFB, MO
MA	104 TFG (ANG)	Massachusetts Air Guard
MB	354 TFW (TAC)	Myrtle Beach AFB, SC
MD	175 TFG (ANG)	Maryland Air Guard
NO	926 TFG (AFRES)	New Orleans NAS, LA
NY	174 TFW (ANG)	New York Air Guard
OS**	25 TFS (PACAF)	Suwon AB, Korea
OT	TAWC (TAC)	Eglin AFB, FL
SU	25 TFS (PACAF)	Suwon, Korea
WA	57 TTW*** (TAC)	Nellis AFB, NV
WI	128 TFW (ANG)	Wisconsin Air Guard
WR	81 TFW (USAFE)	RAF Woodbridge, UK

* ED Codes carried only in 1983.
** In 1985, the 25th TFS switched to SU tail codes.
*** The 57th TTW was known as the 57th FWW prior to 1 October 1977.

The second YA-10 at Edwards in 1973. A mixed bomb load has been mounted for stores carrying tests. Both prototypes rolled out in overall gray, FS 595a color 16473. (Fairchild Republic)

Late in 1973, the #2 prototype was repainted the then-vogue camouflage color gunship gray, 36118. This basic scheme was still worn by this aircraft the following spring for the A-7 flyoff. Note the boarding ladders. The YA-10s carried no internal ladder. (USAF)

A much-modified first prototype seen in late 1974. The GAU-8 30mm gun is mounted below a roughly patched nose; moveable slats are added to the inboard wing section, with fillets (unseen in this view) at the trailing edge of the wing; and ventral airflow-smoothing strakes are placed below the fuselage. (USAF)

7

PREPRODUCTION

The first preproduction airframe in flight with flaps full down at 30 degrees. It is painted overall gunship gray (36118), with a white "1" on the tail identifying it as the first A-10A off the production line. Prototype airframes were ignored in the manufacturer's airframe number sequencing. *(USAF)*

Delivery of the six preproduction A-10As (listed officially on Air Force inventories as YA-10As) began in February 1975. Externally they differed only slightly from the prototypes, incorporating changes developed during early flight testing. The preproduction airframes standardized the leading edge slats and trailing edge fairings which had been fitted to the YA-10s to smooth engine airflow at high angles of attack. They also carried the YA-10's ventral strakes to smooth airflow at the under fuselage bomb racks.

The preproduction wing tips were extended outboard of the ailerons; total span became 57.6 feet compared to the YA-10's 55 feet. The YA-10's 40 degree flap travel was reduced to 30 degrees in preproduction aircraft, allowing shorter flap guides and rails at the trailing edges. Flap travel was later limited to 20 degrees.

Up front, the A-10A's all carried the GAU-8 30mm gun (although #1 flew with an empty cooling jacket on several flights). As a result of tests, the gun was depressed 2° from the horizontal to flatten out firing passes. An automatic elevator pitchdown during firing proved unnecessary and was eliminated.

An operable in-flight refueling receptacle was mounted above the gun; the first prototype had tested refueling formations with KC-135s and KC-97s using a dummy receptacle. Ground turnaround was eased by a single point refueling position in the front of the left main landing gear sponson. Gravity refueling positions were retained above the wing and fuselage tanks as an option.

The front end met with a few other changes. A boarding ladder was added to the left side, saving the pilot a long jump down to the ground (or up to the cockpit!). Opposite the ladder, on the right forward fuselage, provisions were made for a removeable pylon to mount the Pave Penny laser designator. Along the forward fuselage sides, most of the small vents and access panels were revised to suit production equipment and electronics. The single nose landing gear door of the YA-10 was split into two segments.

The preproduction airframes also carried the new "-100" versions of the TF34. Just outside the engines, the vertical tails were reshaped, rounding out the lower leading edge.

The pitot-static system was brought up to production standards, with a pitot boom mounted at the right wing tip.

Each of the preproduction airframes was used in several ways during the test phase, including color scheme experimentation. But the primary test functions of each airframe were as follows:

#1 (664)   Performance and handling quality tests, flutter and air load demonstrations, and load to 100% limit.

#2 (665)   Armament tests, including GAU-8, associated subsystem evaluations, and stores certification tests.

#3 (666)   Subsystem evaluations and weapon delivery accuracy.

#4 (667)   Initial Operational Test and Evaluation (IOT&E) performance and propulsion evaluations.

#5 (668)   IOT&E and stores certification tests.

#6 (669)   Climatic test airframe.

Another view of Airframe #1, this time with a demonstration load of eighteen black and white 500 pound bombs (one rack has been removed from each wing). Note the inverted national insignia below the right wing. The same mistake occurred with the insignia above the left wing.

(Fairchild Republic)

GENERAL ARRANGEMENT

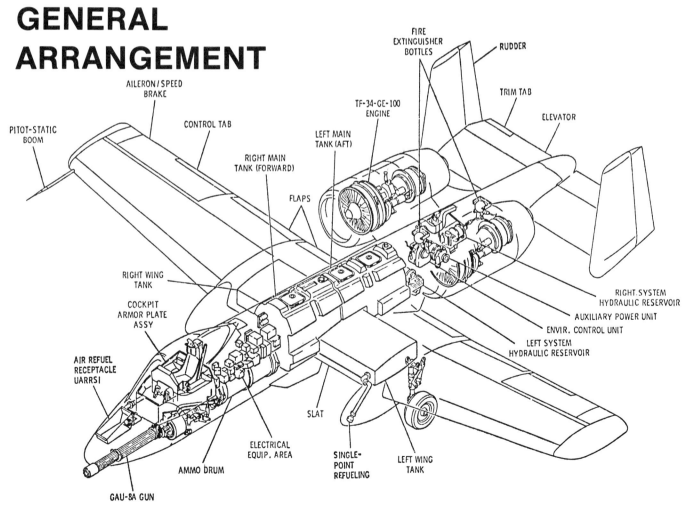

The second preproduction airframe carrying a pair of 2,000 pound smart bombs. Beneath the left wing is a GBU-8 electro-optical (or TV) guided bomb; beneath the right wing is a GBU-10 laser guided bomb. (Fairchild Republic)

Number 2 drops a 500 pound LGB several months later. The aircraft's blotchy appearance results from a scheme with a thin layer of white over a base coat of black. Uneven wearing of the white on high friction areas allows more of the dark base coat to show through.

(Fairchild Republic)

Mission and Description

Navy Equivalent: None   Mfg's Model: A-10

The principal mission of the A-10A is the close support of ground fighting units in support of the attainment of U.S. military objectives over a wide range of possible conflict situations. It is also designed to function in the escort and armed reconnaissance roles.

The A-10A is a single place, highly maneuverable vehicle powered by two turbofan engines and is capable of operating from semi-prepared forward airstrips.

Special features of this airplane are split aileron speed brakes, cockpit protective armor, twin vertical tail, high-lift airfoil, universal air refueling receptable slipway installation, engine location in aft fuselage mounted pods and full triple redundant flight control system.

The fire control system includes a 30mm high velocity gun. Armament controls and displays utilized for identification, selection, arming, firing, monitoring, and selective jettisoning of stores are consolidated into a single control panel. The aircraft serves as a stable aiming platform and has the capability to carry an external store load of up to 16,000 lb. of ordnance on 10 fixed pylons plus an optional centerline station.

The cockpit is provided with 2.75 psi differential pressurization, heating and cooling, jettisonable canopy, zero speed/zero altitude escape seat and anti-G suit provision.

Development

Design Initiated	Jul 70
First Flight (Prototype)	May 72
Contract Approved	Mar 73
First Flight (DT & E)	Dec 74

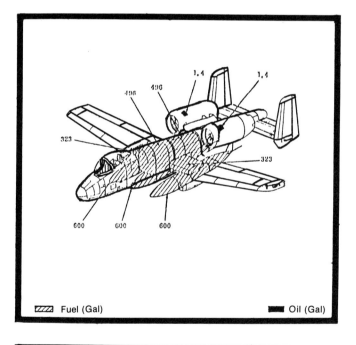

ZZZ Fuel (Gal)   ■ Oil (Gal)

POWER PLANT

No. & Model	(2) TF34 GE-100
Mfr	General Electric
Engine Spec No.	CP45E0002
Type	Axial Flow Turbofan
Length	78.0″
Diameter	44.0″
Weight (dry)	1427 lb
Tall Pipe	Fixed Area Nozzle
Augmentation	None

F U E L

Location	No. Tanks	Gal
Wing, int	2	646
Wing, drop	2	1200
Fus, int*	2	992
Fus, drop	1	600
	Total	3438

* Partial self-sealing

Grade	JP-4
Specification	MIL-T-5624

OIL

Nacelles 2	(tot) 2.8
Specification	MIL-L-7808

WEIGHTS

Loading	Lb	L.F.
Empty	19,856 (E)	
Basic	22,844 (E)	
Design	29,701	7.33
Combat	*38,136	5.85
Max T.O. (overload)	‡ 46,786	4.88
Max T.O. (normal)	† 46,270	4.03
Max Land	† 46,270	4.00

(E)   Estimated

+   For Basic Mission

†   Defined by Air Vehicle Specification

‡   Limited by space

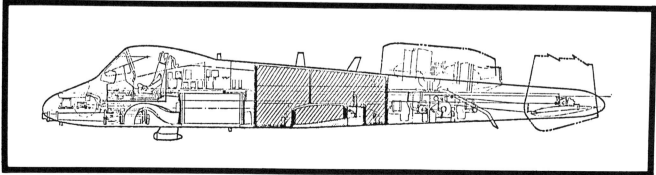

Aircraft #4 flew in an experimental tan paint called "40% MASK 10A". National insignia and markings are black.
(Fairchild Republic)

The last of the preproduction airframes tucks in its landing gear during takeoff from Edwards AFB. Two MERs with six 500 lb. bombs each are under the fuselage, and two TERs with three 500 lb. bombs each are outboard of the wheel sponsons. The unusual color scheme saw three thicknesses of white paint over a black base coat to produce three mottled gray tones.
(USAF)

An unnumbered airframe was used for the fatigue test program. In September 1975, a crack developed after simulating 80% of the aircraft's lifetime. Reinforced, the fuselage went to 6,000 hours without further incident.
(Fairchild Republic)

Loading and Performance - Typical Mission

STANDARD DAY - MIL-C-5011A RULES CONDITIONS				CLOSE AIR SUPPORT I	RECON. MISSION II	ESCORT MISSION III	FERRY MISSION IV
TAKEOFF WEIGHT			(lb)	45,071	45,071	40,269	46,786 (5)
Fuel at 6.5 lb/gal (Grade JP-4)			(lb)	10,650	10,650	10,650	22,350
Payload (Bombs)			(lb)	9540 (3)	9540 (3)	4240 (4)	None
Payload (Ammo)			(lb)	1170 (6)	1170 (6)	2105 (7)	None
Wing Loading			(lb/sq ft)	89.1	89.1	79.6	92.5
Stall Speed (Power Off)			(kn)	103.8	103.8	98.1	105.7
Takeoff Ground Run at S. L.	(1)	(11)	(ft)	1905	1905	1480	2075
Takeoff to Clear 50 Feet	(1)	(11)	(ft)	2760	2760	2120	3025
Rate of Climb at S.L.	(2)		(fpm)	3290	3290	3975	3160
Rate of Climb at S.L. (One Engine Out)	(1)		(fpm)	1115	1115	1520	1055
Time: S.L. to 10,000 Feet	(2)		(min)	-	-	2.9	-
Time: S.L. to 15,000 Feet	(2)		(min)	-	5.9	-	-
Time: S.L. to 25,000 Feet	(2)		(min)	14.0	-	-	14.6
Service Ceiling (100 fpm)	(2)		(ft)	30,500	30,500	34,400	29,900
Service Ceiling (One Engine Out)	(1)		(ft)	14,500	14,500	19,100	14,000
COMBAT RANGE			(n, mi)	-	-	-	3048
Average Cruise Speed			(kn)	-	-	-	296
Initial Cruising Altitude			(ft)	-	-	-	25,000
Final Cruising Altitude			(ft)	-	-	-	35,000
Total Mission Time			(hr)	-	-	-	10.3
COMBAT RADIUS			(n, mi)	250	401	243	-
Average Cruise Speed			(kn)	286	217	173	-
Initial Cruising Altitude			(ft)	25,000	15,000	10,000	-
Final Cruising Altitude			(ft)	35,000	35,000	25,000	-
Total Mission Time			(hr)	3.9	3.8	3.9	-
Loiter Time at 5000 Feet			(min)	116	-	60	-
COMBAT WEIGHT	(9)		(lb)	38,136	39,915	34,532	25,261
Combat Altitude			(ft)	S.L.	S.L.	S.L.	35,000
Combat Speed	(1)		(kn)	376	376	389	390
Combat Climb	(1)		(fpm)	5340	5050	6200	1990
Combat Ceiling (500 fpm)	(1)		(ft)	33,400	32,400	36,600	43,500
Service Ceiling (100 fpm)	(2)		(ft)	34,700	33,500	37,800	43,900
Service Ceiling (One Engine Out)	(2)		(ft)	16,400	14,700	20,700	30,100
Max Rate of Climb at S.L.	(1)		(fpm)	5340	5050	6200	8940
Max Speed at Optimum Alt.	(1)		(kn/ft)	389/10,000	389/10,000	400/10,000	405/15,000
Basic Speed at S.L.	(1)		(kn)	376	376	389	397
LANDING WEIGHT			(lb)	25,077	25,077	24,903	25,261
Ground Roll at S.L.	(10)	(12)	(ft)	890	890	885	895
Total from 50 Feet	(10)	(12)	(ft)	1750	1750	1740	1760

NOTES

(1) Maximum thrust
(2) Intermediate thrust
(3) 18 - MK 82's
(4) 8 - MK-82's

(5) 3 - 600 gal tanks, dropped when empty
(6) 750 rds 30mm, 625 lb expanded
(7) 1350 rds 30mm, 1485 lb expanded
(8) Deleted

(9) Immediately prior to combat
(10) Anti-skid braking
(11) 20" flaps
(12) 30" flaps

A-10 COCKPIT

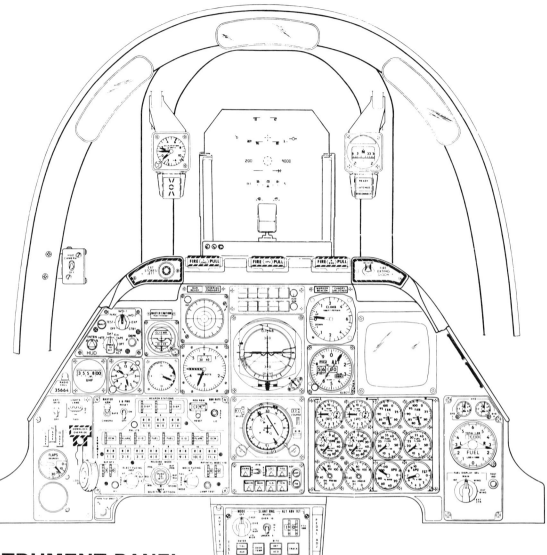

INSTRUMENT PANEL (TYPICAL)

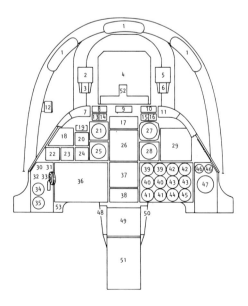

1. Rear View Mirrors
2. Accelerometer
3. Angle of Attack indexers
4. Head Up Display (HUD)
5. Standby Compass
6. Air Refuel Status Lights
7. External Stores Jettison Switch
8. Left Engine Fire Pull Handle
9. APU Fire Pull Handle
10. Right Engine Fire Pull Handle
11. Fire Extinguishing Agent Discharge Switch
12. Gun Camera Switch
13. Gun Ready Light
14. Nose Wheel Steering Engaged Light
15. Marker Beacon Light
16. Canopy Unlocked Light
17. RHAW Control Indicator
18. HUD Control Panel
19. Master Caution Light
20. Standby Attitude Indicator

21. RHAW Azimuth Indicator
22. UHF Remote Chan/Freq Indicator
23. Clock
24. Angle of Attack Indicator
25. Airspeed Indicator
26. Attitude Director Indicator (ADI)
27. Vertical Velocity Indicator
28. Altimeter
29. TV Monitor
30. Anti-Skid Switch
31. Landing/Taxi Lights Switch
32. Landing Gear Position Display
33. Landing Gear Handle and Override Button
34. Flap Position Indicator
35. Deleted
36. Armament Control Panel
37. Horizontal Situation Indicator (HSI)
38. Navigation Mode Select Panel
39. Interstage Turbine Temperature Indicator (L&R)
40. Engine Core Speed Indicator (L & R)
41. Engine Oil Pressure Indicator (L & R)
42. Fan Speed Indicator (L & R)
43. Fuel Flow Indicator
44. APU Tachometer
45. APU Temperature Indicator
46. Hydraulic Pressure Gauge (Left Sys & Right Sys)
47. Fuel Quantity Indicator
48. Auxiliary Landing Gear Extension Handle
49. Laser Spot Seeker Panel
50. Rudder Pedal Adjustment Handle
51. Essential Circuit Breaker Panel
52. Gun Camera CTVS
53. HARS Fast Erect Switch

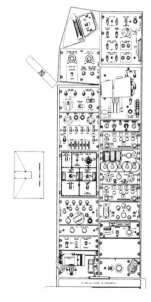

Instrument panel for serial number 78-589 (the 209th A-10A) during production at the Hagerstown facility.
(Fairchild Republic)

RIGHT CONSOLE (TYPICAL)

1. CAUTION LIGHT PANEL
2. CANOPY CONTROL SWITCH
3. CANOPY JETTISON HANDLE
4. BOARDING LADDER EXTENSION BUTTON
5. CHAFF/FLARE CONTROL PANEL
6. ECM PANEL
7. ELECTRICAL POWER PANEL
8. ILS CONTROL PANEL
9. TACAN CONTROL PANEL
10. MANUAL CANOPY OPENING ASSIST HANDLE
11. OXYGEN CONTROL PANEL
12. ENVIRONMENT CONTROL PANEL
13. CANOPY BREAKER TOOL
14. CANOPY ACTUATOR DISENGAGE LEVER
15. SAFETY PIN STOWAGE
16. HARS CONTROL PANEL
17. LIGHTING CONTROL PANEL
18. OXYGEN HOSE AND INTERCOM CONNECTION
19. FLIGHT DATA STOWAGE
20. CONTROL DISPLAY UNIT (CDU)

LEFT CONSOLE (TYPICAL)

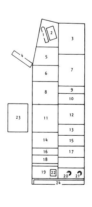

1. EMERGENCY BRAKE HANDLE
2. SEAT HEIGHT ADJUSTMENT SWITCH
3. FUEL SYSTEM CONTROL PANEL
4. MANUAL CANOPY OPENING ASSIST HANDLE
5. AUXILIARY LIGHTING CONTROL PANEL
6. STABILITY AUGMENTATION SYSTEM PANEL (SAS)
7. THROTTLE QUADRANT
8. IFF CONTROL PANEL
9. TV MONITOR CONTROL PANEL
10. VHF/AM RADIO CONTROL PANEL

11. EMERGENCY FLIGHT CONTROL PANEL
12. UHF RADIO CONTROL PANEL
13. VHF/FM RADIO CONTROL PANEL
14. INTERCOM CONTROL PANEL
15. CIPHONY PANEL
16. STALL WARNING CONTROL PANEL
17. CTVS/AVTR CONTROL PANEL
18. ANTENNA SELECT PANEL
19. UTILITY LIGHT
20. ANTI-G SUIT VALVE TEST BUTTON
21. ANTI-G SUIT HOSE
22. ARMAMENT OVERRIDE SWITCH
23. PIDDLE PAK STOWAGE
24. PIDDLE PAK DISPOSAL

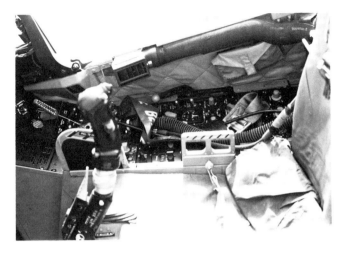

(Top) Left and right side consoles in the cockpit of a production A-10A. The single handle on the right releases the inertia lock for the pilot's harness to improve cockpit freedom. Dual handles at either side of the control column are the ACES II ejection handles: pulling one (or both) removes the pilot from the aircraft. (Van Winkle)

Right side of a preproduction airframe cockpit, 1975. The seat is the ESCAPAC. (USAF)

Under-canopy decking behind the ACES II seat. (Van Winkle)

PRODUCTION AIRFRAMES

Early production airframes prepare for takeoff at Hagerstown. 75-278 wears an asymetrical color scheme of 30% and 50% MASK-10A paint with black markings. The other three aircraft have slightly different values of the two paints in a graded scheme with 36118 gunship gray markings.

(Fairchild Republic)

The first production A-10A flew in October 1975, but deliveries to TAC were delayed for five months. The elimination of four preproduction airframes by Congress overlooked the Air Force's legitimate need to evaluate the aircraft. The "let's-buy-one-aeroplane-and-let-all-the-aviators-take-turns" approach couldn't work, so the four initial production planes took part of the load.

In March 1976, TAC received its first A-10A. From then on the story of the A-10 becomes a listing of operational events: the first European deployment in September, adverse weather missions in Washington in November and Alaska in January 1977, surge test at Nellis in February, first RED FLAG exercise in April. In exercise after exercise TAC refined its tactics with the aircraft. By 1978, tactics had made the A-10 less vulnerable to ground-based threats than originally expected, so the camouflage was changed for better defense against enemy fighters.

TAC's first operational unit was the 354th TFW, which received its first aircraft in March of 1977. In January 1979, the 81st TFW received USAFE's first A-10s. The strong threat to Europe from Soviet armor made the 81st the only USAF wing to have six combat squadrons. In April, the Connecticut ANG got its first A-10s, marking the first time an Air National Guard unit acquired a fighter that had not been handed down from a regular USAF unit. In June 1980, the first AFRES A-10 was delivered to Barksdale AFB, Louisiana. For PACAF, the Korean-based 25th TFS began getting A-10s in November 1981, and the Alaskan Air Command's 18th TFS followed the next month. (MAC and SAC are the only USAF combat commands not flying A-10s!).

Of course there are problems in every aircraft's development, but the one most mentioned about the A-10 came up on 3 April 1978. At a ceremony marking the delivery of the 100th airframe, the name "Thunderbolt II" was officially bestowed upon the A-10. Two red script "Thunderbolt II" decals were stuck on the side of serial 75-553 that morning, and removed about an hour after the ceremony. The nickname didn't stick any better than the decal, especially around aircrews who had been using "Warthog" since 1975.

An early production airframe in asymetrical camouflage - dark beneath the left wing and light below the right. The left engine nacelle has the usual stain from the auxiliary power unit exhaust. Flap guides are to production standards.

(USAF)

Speed brakes are full open for landing at Bicycle Lake, California, during RED FLAG exercises in April 1977. A training Maverick hangs below the wing.

(USAF)

A pair of 354th TFW Warthogs over the Atlantic near their home base in 1977. The graded production camouflage has been altered only by the addition of black unit and command shields, "MB" tail codes, and three-digit wheel sponson markings.

(USAF)

A New York ANG A-10 seen shortly after "The Boys From Syracuse" returned from training in Europe in 1982. The yellow lion and "Bravaria" title on the right nose were worn in honor of the 174th TFG's regular home during NATO deployments. The final production camouflage substitutes 36081 for the 36118.

(Linn)

A-10A ANTENNA LOCATIONS & SYSTEMS

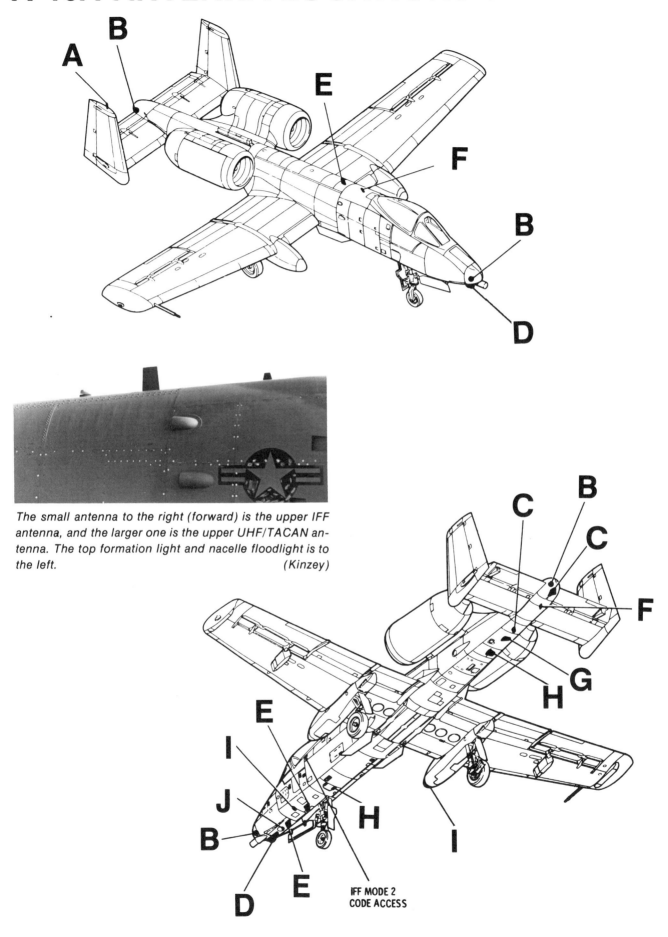

The small antenna to the right (forward) is the upper IFF antenna, and the larger one is the upper UHF/TACAN antenna. The top formation light and nacelle floodlight is to the left. (Kinzey)

IFF MODE 2
CODE ACCESS

(A) AN/UPN-25 X-Band radar. A single antenna post mounted atop the right tail fin to increase the A-10's visibility to ground or air based radar controllers. Mounted on all serials, but removed in the field from several examples.

(B) AN/ALR-69 Radar warning system. Four small nodes, two on either side of the nose and two on either side of the tail, provide warning against radar detection and tracking. Also, two tail antenna as noted in (C). Mounted only on serials 78-582 and subsequent.

(C) Radar warning system. Two antenna beneath the tail serve different systems, depending on the aircraft serial number. Prior to 75-299 (unless upgraded to ALR-64) the ALR-46(V) was mounted. From 75-299 through 76-554 (unless upgraded to ALR-64) the ALR-46A is carried. From 77-177 through 77-276 (plus any previous serials as modified) the antenna serve the ALR-64. All serials from 78-582 mount the ALR-69, with no modding of prior airframes. Some airframes have deleted the aftermost of these two antennas.

(D) Radar warning system. On airframes prior to 78-582 (those carrying ALR-46(V), ALR-46A, or ALR-64 above), a single antenna under the nose to the right of the GAU-8 muzzle to give forward warning. This antenna was omitted with the introduction of ALR-69.

(E) AN/ARC-164(V) UHF radio and AN/ARN-118(V) TACAN. A single knifeblade antenna behind the canopy and one below the nose serve both ultra-high frequency two-way communications and the TACAN navigation system. The lower antenna is mounted in one of two positions: beside the nose wheel door for serials prior to 78-622 or a few feet further aft for serials 78-622 and subsequent.

(F) AN/APX-101 IFF (Identification, Friend or Foe). When switched on, a small antenna behind the canopy and one below the tail serve as transponders when interrogated by external radar systems. All serials.

(G) VHF/AM Radio. A single antenna beneath the rear fuselage serves two-way communications. For serials prior to 78-626 this involves the Wilcox 807A radio. Serials 78-626 and subsequent mount an AN/ARC-186(V) preset on AM.

(H) VHF/FM Radio and Homing. A single antenna forward of the VHF/AM antenna serves two-way communications on the frequency modulation band. A second 'towel rack' antenna behind the nose gear allows the set to home in VHF/FM signals. Serials prior to 78-626 were loaded with the FM-622A. Serials 78-626 and subsequent carry a second AN/ARC-186(V) preset on FM. (An additional "antenna" mounted on the lower rear fuselage is actually a fuel dump. It is the only protuberance in the area which is not mounted on the aircraft's centerline.)

(I) AN/ARN-108 ILS (Instrument Landing System). The ILS, mounted in serials 77-259 and subsequent, consists of three antennas. The localizer and the glide slope receivers are mounted in the "kneecap" of the right landing gear pod, and the marker beacon receiver is mounted off the centerline beneath the nose.

(J) OA-8697A/ARD UHF/ADF (Automatic Direction Finder). A single antenna, a flush disc below the gun intake, gives bearings on selected stations which are transmitting on UHF.

From left to right are the VHF/FM antenna, fuel dump mast, and VHF/AM antenna under the tail. This view is from the left side. *(Kinzey)*

Close-up of tail showing the two round radar warning antennas with the tail position and strobe light in between. The large antenna fairing under the tail is also a radar warning antenna. *(Kinzey)*

AILERON DETAIL

(Top, left) The left aileron in neutral position. Note the uneven sit and trailing edge pitchup.

(Center, left) Aileron full up for banking turns.

(Left) Aileron full down.

(Top, right) Speed brakes full open, a position only used on the ground. Note the speed brake hinge line, partway thru the chord of the aileron.

(Above) Speed brakes at 80%, the maximum open position in flight.

Left aileron in neutral position. Note the fixed 15° upward pitch of the outboard tab. The moveable inboard geared/servo tab is indexed to 35° on serials 75-266 and subsequent, or to 30° on earlier aircraft.

The same aileron, split open as a speed brake. (The combination aileron/speed brake is called a "deceleron" by the company and crews.) The moveable trim tab is part of the upper deceleron half, with a corresponding cutout in the lower half.

LADDER DETAIL

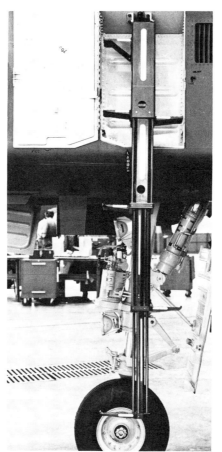

The three boarding ladders used to date are (left) the original ladder of square cross-section, (center) a multi-tubed ladder mounted only on the last twenty production airframes, and (right) a new tubular ladder being retrofitted at depot.

(Left and right Van Winkle, center author)

LEADING EDGE SLAT DETAIL

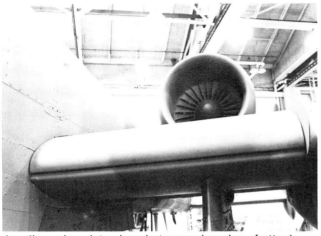

Leading edge slats closed at normal angles of attack.
(USAF)

Slats opened to prevent engine compressor blade stall at high angles of attack.
(USAF)

FLAP DETAIL

Wing flaps, full up.
(USAF)

Wing flaps at 7 degrees; takeoff setting.
(USAF)

Wing flaps full down at 20 degrees; landing setting.
(USAF)

24

REFUELING RECEPTACLE

The unpainted metal in-flight refueling door, with black and white "H" refueling target.

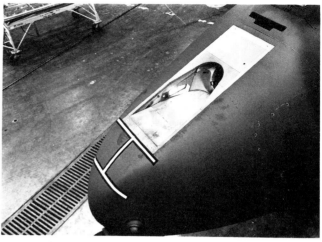

The refueling door slips forward and hinges down to open the fuel intake. The slipway lights are manually controlled from the cockpit.

LIGHTING

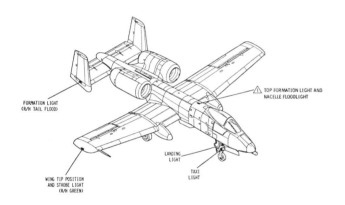

FORMATION LIGHT
(R/H TAIL FLOOD)

TOP FORMATION LIGHT AND
NACELLE FLOODLIGHT

WING TIP POSITION
AND STROBE LIGHT
(R/H GREEN)

LANDING
LIGHT

TAXI
LIGHT

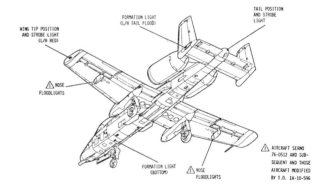

WING TIP POSITION
AND STROBE LIGHT
(L/H RED)

FORMATION LIGHT
(L/H TAIL FLOOD)

TAIL POSITION
AND STROBE
LIGHT

NOSE
FLOODLIGHTS

FORMATION LIGHT
(BOTTOM)

NOSE
FLOODLIGHTS

AIRCRAFT SERNO
76-0512 AND SUB-
SEQUENT AND THOSE
AIRCRAFT MODIFIED
BY T.O. 1A-10-596

Floodlights inside wing racks 1 and 11 illuminate the nose during night refueling operations.

The dorsal formation light doubles as a rearward facing floodlight. The light was moved from between the antenna for unobstructed flooding of the nacelles and tail.

Close-up of right wing tip light. (Kinzey)

LANDING GEAR DETAIL

Nose gear viewed from the front left. *(Van Winkle)*

Forward portion of nose gear well. *(Kinzey)*

Nose gear viewed from the right. *(Kinzey)*

View looking up into the nose gear well. *(Kinzey)*

Right front view of the right main landing gear. (Kinzey)

Inside the left main gear.   *(Van Winkle)*

Left main gear well viewed from the front.   *(Kinzey)*

Three-quarter front view of the left main gear.

EJECTION SEAT

The initial ejection system installed on the A-10 was the Douglas ESCAPAC 1E-9. Beginning with aircraft serial 77-177 the McDonnell ACES II (Advanced Concept Ejection Seat) was mounted, a seat which was eventually retrofitted to all existing Warthogs. The A-10's ACES II is almost identical to the version used on the F-15, although the Eagle does not have canopy breakers. Modelers will recognize the ACES II by its thicker seat frame, its paired ejection handles on either side, and its downward slanting pitot 'horns' atop the headrest.

The pitot system is linked to a seat computer system which automatically determines the ejection mode. As the seat rises out of the cockpit into the slipstream, the pitot system senses speed and altitude. For low speed and altitude, Mode 1 puts the pilot under the silk as quickly as possible. At higher speeds, Mode 2 deploys a drogue chute to slow the pilot and seat for a second longer. (Mode 3 is a high altitude sequence which keeps the pilot in the seat until the drogue brings him to an altitude safe enough for chute deployment. Mode 3 is unnecessary on the A-10 !) The ACES II's computer will also sense an inverted ejection and automatically right the seat before pilot-seat separation.

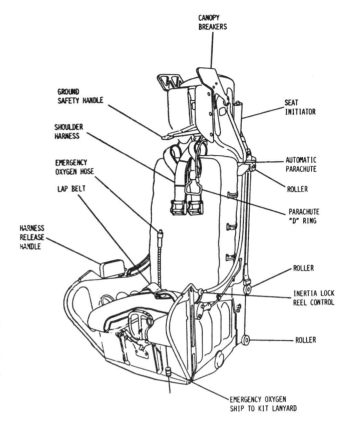

ESCAPAC 1E-9

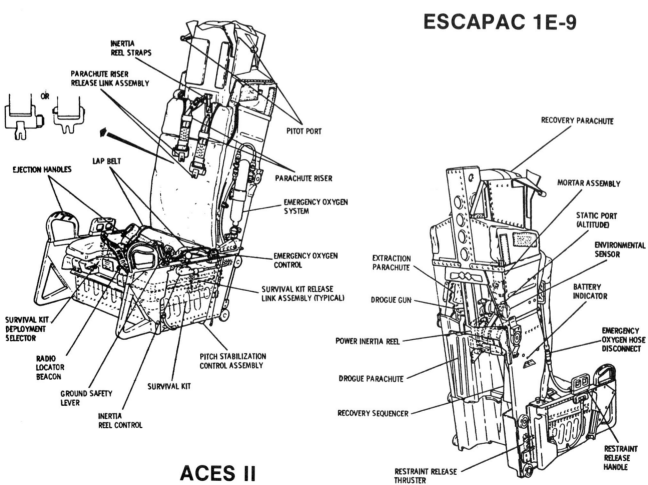

ACES II

On 8 June 1978, Major Francis C. Gideon, Jr. was forced to eject from preproduction aircraft #669 after tests of a new gun propellant led to the shutdown of both engines. A motion picture cameraman in an Edwards chase plane recorded the remarkable footage from which these stills were taken. The seat used was the Douglas IE-9 ESCAPAC. *(USAF)*

The ejection sequence begins as the canopy is blown away from the cockpit. *(USAF)*

The seat rises to the end of its rail under rocket power. *(USAF)*

Clear of the aircraft, the rocket's flame erupts at the rear of the seat. *(USAF)*

As the main rocket sputters out, a mortar atop the seat launches the main canopy's drogue chute. *(USAF)*

The main parachute inflates, breaking the pilot's forward motion. *(USAF)*

N/AW A-10

The N/AW A-10 over the California desert, soon after arriving at Edwards AFB in 1979. The small cartoon on the nose is an owl with a GAU-8 and an umbrella.
(Fairchild Republic)

The Air Force's original concept for the A-X contained a stipulation that the aircraft be capable of modification to a two-seater to handle enhanced electronic systems. In 1978, Fairchild Republic leased back the first preproduction airframe to produce a prototype with night and adverse weather (N/AW) capabilities. Costs of the two-seat project were split, with the company paying $2 million and the Department of Defense paying $5 million. The prototype was listed in Air Force inventories as the YA-10B, but it was known universally as the N/AW A-10.

The second seat was raised, giving the weapons system operator clear forward visibility comparable with the pilot's. To save weight, the bathtub armor was not extended to the rear cockpit. For added stability, the vertical tail was extended twenty inches, but in production this figure would have been only six to eight inches.

Electronics included a Litton LN-39 inertial navigation

system and dual Honeywell APN-194 radar altimeters. Under the left wing, a Westinghouse WX/50 ground mapping radar/moving target indicator was mounted. Production plans were to move this unit to the left wheel sponson. A Texas Instruments AAR-42 forward-looking infrared (FLIR) system was podded under the fuselage, but this would have moved to the right sponson in production. A G.E. low-light-level TV supplemented the FLIR for poor infrared conditions. The Pave Penny was retained, and some experimentation was done with an AVQ-26 Pave Tack laser designator.

Everything worked, but the Air Force was not convinced of its need for the aircraft. Much of the testing went toward development of N/AW capabilities for a single-seat aircraft. Fairchild proposed a two-seat trainer, but the A-10 was simple enough that pilots didn't need two seat transition time. The A-10B never saw production; its prototype is still at Edwards.

Speed brakes open, the N/AW A-10 lands at Edwards. External electronics have not yet been mounted.

(Fairchild Republic)

Right side of the N/AW, showing open electronics bays.

(Van Winkle)

Nose of the only two-seater, with canopies closed. Both canopies came from the same mold, with the rear one cut to fit.

(Van Winkle)

Sideways hinging canopies had also been suggested for the A-10A to save weight, but the concept was dropped before hitting the production line.

(Van Winkle)

FLIR mounted on the centerline, with the radar pod under the left wing.

(Van Winkle)

The vertical tail was extended twenty inches for lateral stability. *(Van Winkle)*

Pave Penny mount on the N/AW. *(Van Winkle)*

Top view against the desert floor. Color scheme is overall 36118 gunship gray. *(Fairchild Republic)*

A-10 COLORS

Airframe 75-274 of the 333rd TFTS, 355th TTW. 1980. *(Wally Van Winkle)*

Washdown of s/n 75-304 at Davis-Monthan. 367th TFTS, 355th TTW, June 1980. *(Wally Van Winkle)*

The Wisconsin ANG's 176th TASS became the 176th TFS when the squadron converted from OA-37s in 1982.

(Wally Van Winkle)

Photographed at Davis-Monthan, this 81st TFW Warthog wears an early two-tone gray scheme. Part of a false canopy painted beneath the fuselage carries over onto the open nose wheel door. *(Brian C. Rogers via Van Winkle)*

A red diagonal tail band marks the squadron leader's aircraft for the 353d TFS, 354th TFW. This photograph was taken in Egypt during Operation BRIGHT STAR, 1980. *(USAF)*

The second YA-10 was fitted with parts of a GAU-8 gun and painted in an approximation of the standard A-10 camouflage scheme for public tours with the Air Force's Orientation Group. 1979. *(David W. Menard)*

"The Boys From Syracuse" marks the engine pods of 174th TFW (NYANG) A-10As. (s/n 78-652) *(USAF)*

An echelon of 103d TFG (CTANG) A-10As in 1979.*(USAF)*

The first preproduction A-10A was modified into a two-seat Night/Adverse Weather prototype in 1979. Official USAF inventories list the aircraft as the YA-10B.

(Fairchild Republic)

A 422d FWS A-10A wearing one of the experimental camouflages evaluated during exercise JAWS II. April 1978.

(Mick Roth)

The first 'lizard' scheme was tested on 75-269. Note the light gray initially evaluated in combination with two greens. The photo was taken in July 1980. *(Wally Van Winkle)*

A 355th TTW Warthog lands at Davis-Monthan.

(Brian C. Rogers via Van Winkle)

The fourth preproduction airframe being towed at Edwards AFB, May, 1980. *(Wally Van Winkle)*

ENGINE COLORS

(Top) A General Electric TF34-100 engine awaits installation on a 357th TFTS A-10A in May 1982. (Rob Stern)

(Right) Details of the underside of the right engine on a 354th TFW Warthog. Left and right engines are interchangeable. (Wally Van Winkle)

(Below) With an engine hoist attached to the top of the nacelle, a TF34 is raised to its position in a 357th TFTS aircraft. (Rob Stern)

Instrument panel of s/n 75-267. 1981. (Wally Van Winkle)

Rear deck, canopy rails, and Escapac ejection seat details.
(USAF)

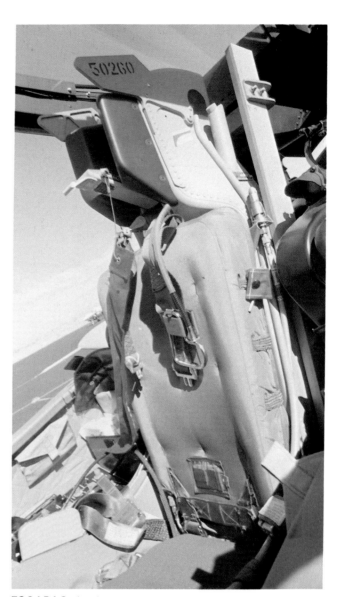

ESCAPAC ejection seat details. The serial number (75-260) is painted on the canopy breaker atop the seat. (Kinzey)

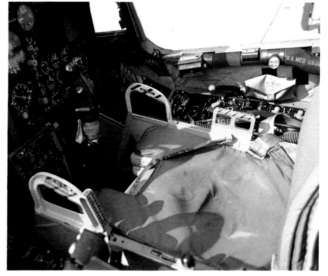

These two photos show the ACES II seat installed in an A-10. The ACES II is now the standard ejection seat in the Warthog, replacing the ESCAPAC seat shown above.

(Top) A practice AGM-65B (scene magnification TV seeker) Maverick is seen mounted on a 355th TFW aircraft.
(Rob Stern)

(Right) The LAU-88 missile rail holds up to three AGM-65s.
(Wally Van Winkle)

(Below right) The Pave Penny laser seeker pod is a passive laser designator. (Wally Van Winkle)

(Below left) Laser scoring device mounted on the gun of a 57th TTW A-10. Note the nickname, "Excalibur".
(Kurt Minert)

(Above) ALQ-119 electronic countermeasures pod mounted on 75-265. The pod is always mounted in a forward position on the wing rack to avoid interfering with open speed brakes. (Wally Van Winkle)

Flare dispenser (covered), integrally mounted at the trailing point of each landing gear pod. (Wally Van Winkle)

Flare dispenser (covered) and wingtip navigation light. (Wally Van Winkle)

Tail warning radar receivers and (center) navigation light. (Wally Van Winkle)

The Air Force Reserves' 45th TFS (Indiana) received its first Warthogs in 1981. *(John P. Santucci via Van Winkle)*

The second preproduction airframe as photographed in 1983. The AFSC insignia tops the "AD" tail codes used by the Armament Development Center. *(Wally Van Winkle)*

The nose of a second TAWC A-10 (s/n 82-538), with additional radar warning nodes mounted above the GAU-8 muzzles. *(Wally Van Winkle)*

An A-10 of the Alaskan Air Command's 18th TFS at McChord AFB, WA, in 1983. Two 600 gallon ferry tanks hang below the fuselage. *(Remington via Van Winkle)*

This A-10A (s/n 79-166) of the Tactical Air Warfare Center at Eglin AFB carries an ALQ-131 ECM pod under its right wing. *(Wally Van Winkle)*

DIMENSIONS

MEASUREMENT	ACTUAL	1/144th SCALE	1/100th SCALE	1/72nd SCALE	1/48th SCALE
Wing Span	57' 6"	4.79"	6.90"	9.58"	14.38"
Horiz. Tail Span	18' 10"	1.57"	2.26"	3.14"	4.71"
Overall Length	53' 4"	4.44"	6.40"	8.89"	13.33"
Wheel Tread	14' 8"	1.22"	1.76"	2.44"	3.67"
Wheel Base	17' 8.76"	1.48"	2.13"	2.95"	4.43"
Height (Fin)	9' 8"	.81"	1.16"	1.61"	2.42"
Fuselage Length	52' 6"	4.38"	6.30"	8.75"	13.13"
Fuselage Width	4' 5"	.37"	.53"	.74"	1.10"

AREAS

Wings (including flaps and ailerons) ..... 506 sq. ft.
Flaps (total) .... 85.99 sq. ft.
Ailerons (total, including tabs) ...... 47.54 sq. ft.
Speed brakes (total) .... 86.78 sq. ft.
Leading Edge Slats (2) .... 10.56 sq. ft.
Horizontal Tail (including elevators) ..... 118.4 sq. ft.
Elevators (total, including tabs) ...... 29.0 sq. ft.
Fin (including rudder) .... 107.5 sq. ft.
Rudder (total, including tabs) .... 23.5 sq. ft.

DETAIL & SCALE, INC.

$\dfrac{1}{72\text{ND}}$ ─── SCALE

® FIVE-VIEW DRAWING

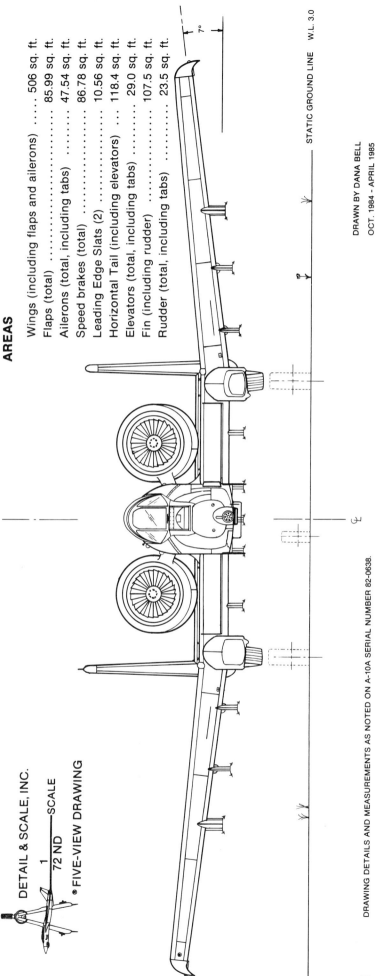

STATIC GROUND LINE   W.L. 3.0

DRAWN BY DANA BELL
OCT. 1984 - APRIL 1985

DRAWING DETAILS AND MEASUREMENTS AS NOTED ON A-10A SERIAL NUMBER 82-0638.

FIVE-VIEW DRAWINGS

DETAIL & SCALE, INC.

$\frac{1}{72 \text{ ND}}$ ——SCALE

® FIVE-VIEW DRAWING

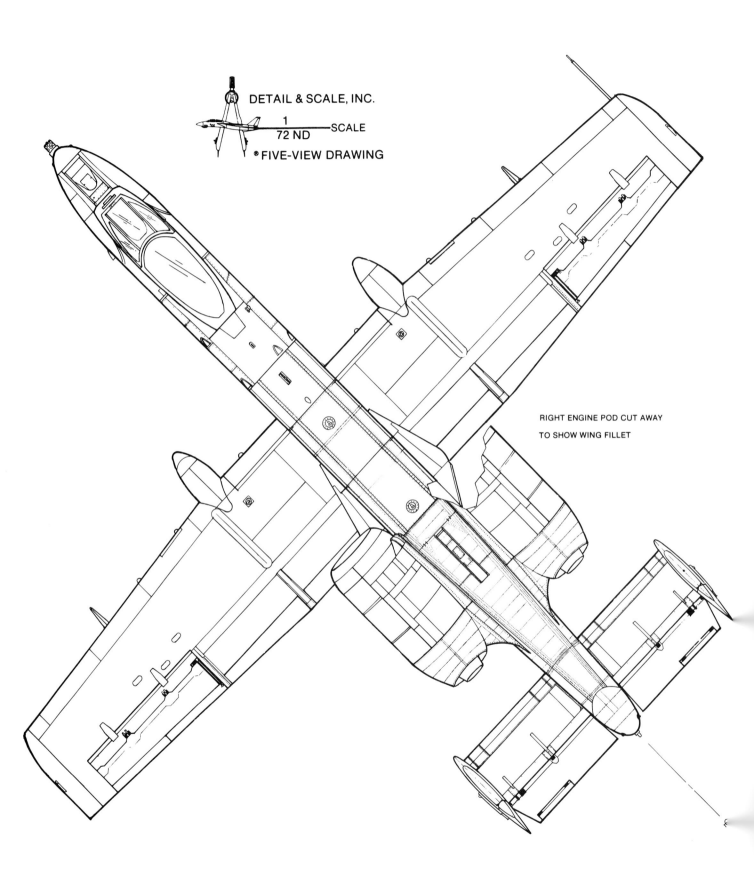

RIGHT ENGINE POD CUT AWAY

TO SHOW WING FILLET

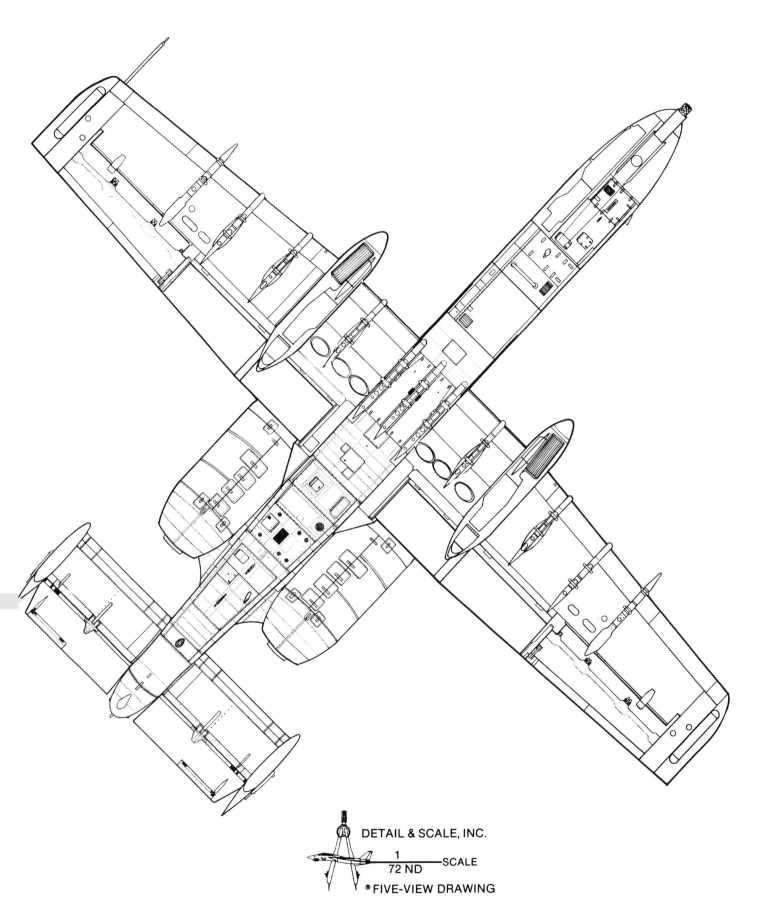

DETAIL & SCALE, INC.

$$\frac{1}{72\text{ ND}}$$ ——SCALE

® FIVE-VIEW DRAWING

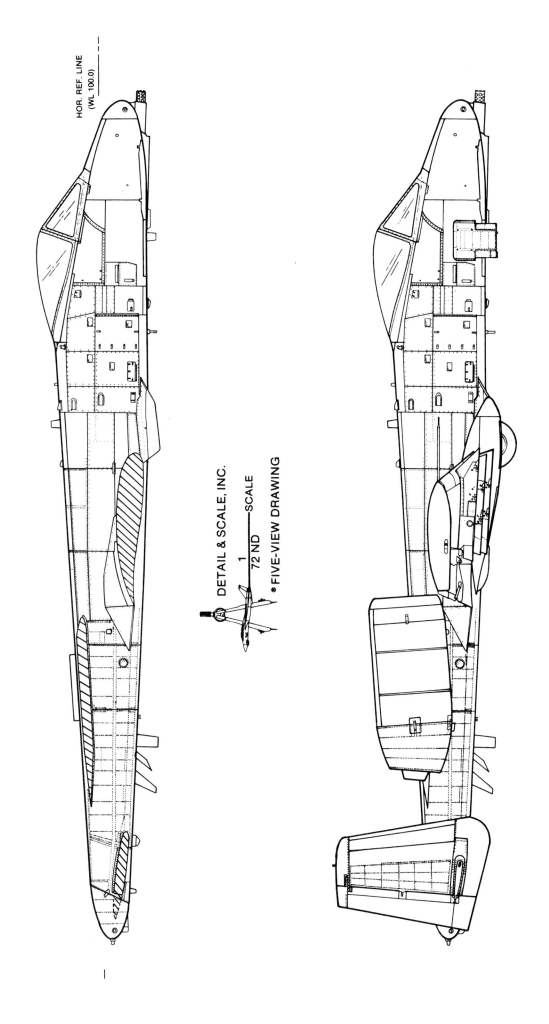

HOR. REF. LINE
(WL 100.0)

DETAIL & SCALE, INC.

1
——— SCALE
72 ND

●FIVE-VIEW DRAWING

44

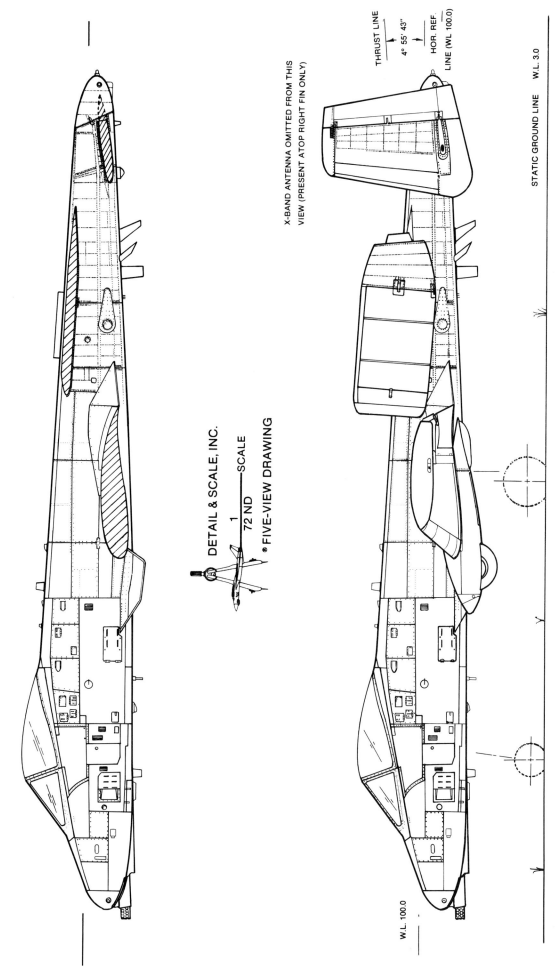

X-BAND ANTENNA OMITTED FROM THIS
VIEW (PRESENT ATOP RIGHT FIN ONLY)

THRUST LINE

4° 55' 43"

HOR. REF.
LINE (WL 100.0)

STATIC GROUND LINE   W.L. 3.0

UNDERWING RACKS OMITTED FROM THIS VIEW FOR CLARITY.

W.L. 100.0

DETAIL & SCALE, INC.

1
——— SCALE
72 ND

® FIVE-VIEW DRAWING

ACCESS DOORS & INSPECTION PANELS

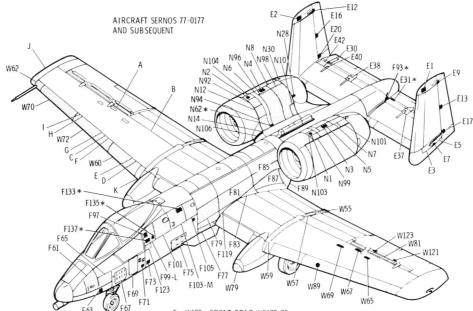

AIRCRAFT SERNOS 77-0177
AND SUBSEQUENT

A - W50, W78 - REAR SPAR, WS241.50
(AILERON REMOVED)
B - W76, W136, W138, W140, W142 - REAR
SPAR BETWEEN WS117.27 AND WS241.50
(FLAPS LOWERED)
C - W18 - FRONT SPAR BETWEEN WS110 AND WS190
(W72 REMOVED)
D - W96 - FRONT SPAR WS139.25
(W60 REMOVED)
E - W98 - FRONT SPAR WS147.07
(W60 REMOVED)

F - W100 - FRONT SPAR WS189.90
(W72 REMOVED)
G - W102 - FRONT SPAR WS191.14
(W72 REMOVED)
H - W104 - FRONT SPAR WS224.25
(W72 REMOVED)
I - W106 - FRONT SPAR WS237.32
(W72 REMOVED)
J - W108, W126 - BORESIGHT COVER ACCESS
(WING TIP EXTENSION REMOVED)
K - W20 - AFT OF MID SPAR IN RIGHT
LANDING GEAR POD

L - TWO QUICK-RELEASE DOORS IN F99 FOR
PRE-SETTING IFF MODE 4 AND SECURE
VOICE (AIRCRAFT 77-0177 AND
SUBSEQUENT)

M - QUICK-RELEASE DOOR IN F103 FOR
PRE-SETTING IFF MODE 2 (AIRCRAFT
77-0177 AND SUBSEQUENT)

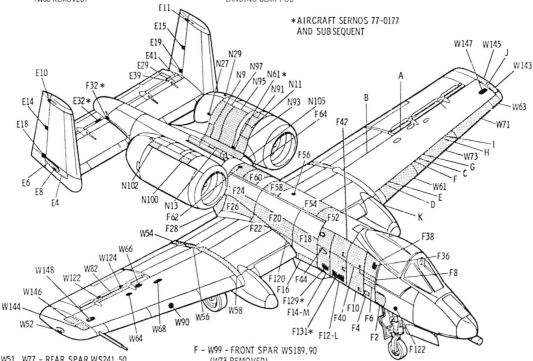

*AIRCRAFT SERNOS 77-0177
AND SUBSEQUENT

A - W51, W77 - REAR SPAR WS241.50
(AILERON REMOVED)
B - W75, W135, W137, W139, W141 - REAR SPAR
BETWEEN WS117.27 AND WS241.50
(FLAPS LOWERED)
C - W17 - FRONT SPAR BETWEEN WS110 AND WS 190
(W73 REMOVED)
D - W95 - FRONT SPAR WS139.25
(W61 REMOVED)
E - W97 - FRONT SPAR WS147.07
(W61 REMOVED)

F - W99 - FRONT SPAR WS189.90
(W73 REMOVED)
G - W101 - FRONT SPAR WS191.14
(W73 REMOVED)
H - W103 - FRONT SPAR WS224.25
(W73 REMOVED)
I - W105 - FRONT SPAR WS237.32
(W73 REMOVED)
J - W107, W125 - (BORESIGHT COVER ACCESS)
(WINGTIP EXTENSION REMOVED)
K - W19 - AFT OF MID SPAR IN LEFT
MAIN LANDING GEAR POD

L - TWO QUICK-RELEASE DOORS IN F12 FOR
PRE-SETTING IFF MODE 4 AND SECURE
VOICE (AIRCRAFT 77-0177 AND
SUBSEQUENT)

M - QUICK-RELEASE DOOR IN F14 FOR
PRE-SETTING IFF MODE 2 (AIRCRAFT
77-0177 AND SUBSEQUENT)

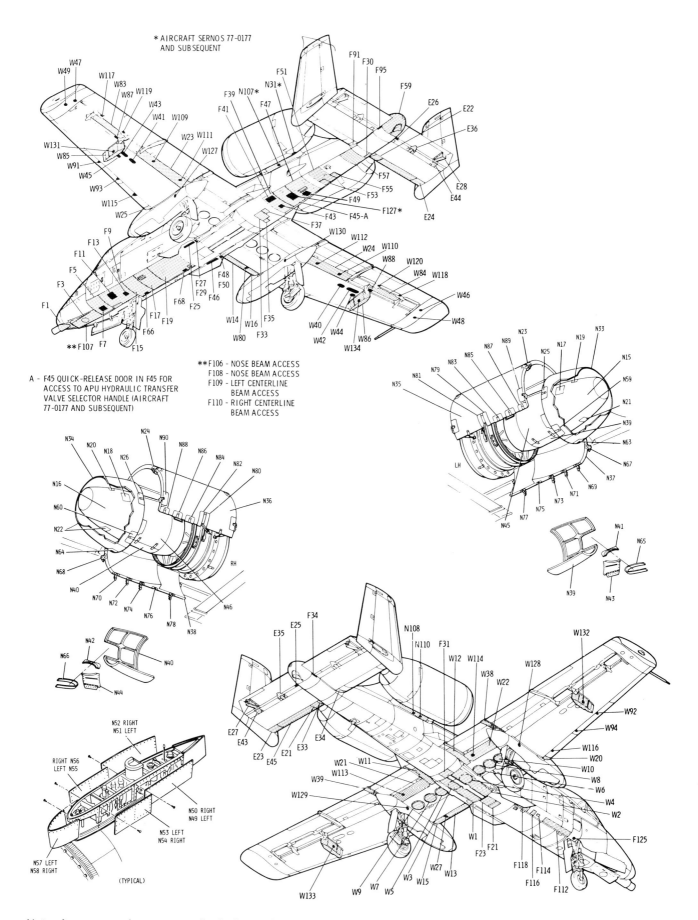

* AIRCRAFT SERNOS 77-0177
AND SUBSEQUENT

A - F45 QUICK-RELEASE DOOR IN F45 FOR
ACCESS TO APU HYDRAULIC TRANSFER
VALVE SELECTOR HANDLE (AIRCRAFT
77-0177 AND SUBSEQUENT)

** F106 - NOSE BEAM ACCESS
   F108 - NOSE BEAM ACCESS
   F109 - LEFT CENTERLINE
          BEAM ACCESS
   F110 - RIGHT CENTERLINE
          BEAM ACCESS

Note: Access panels are generally designated with odd numbers on the left side of the aircraft and even numbers on the right. Prefix letters designate Wing, Fuselage, Nacelle, or Empennage.

47

Open panels F-61 and F-65 hang from lightweight web straps on the left forward fuselage. The bay on the left holds the inverter battery relay box, while the battery is stored in the right bay.

Aircraft carrying the inertial navigation system (INS) can be recognized by a small 'periscope' air intake at the canopy's right rear corner. An exhaust port has been added just aft of the intake.

The ground-operated ejection handle, behind door F-73.

Details of the single-point refueling position located in the "kneecap" (panel W-79) on the left wheel sponson.
(Left: Marshall; right: author)

AIRCRAFT STATIONS

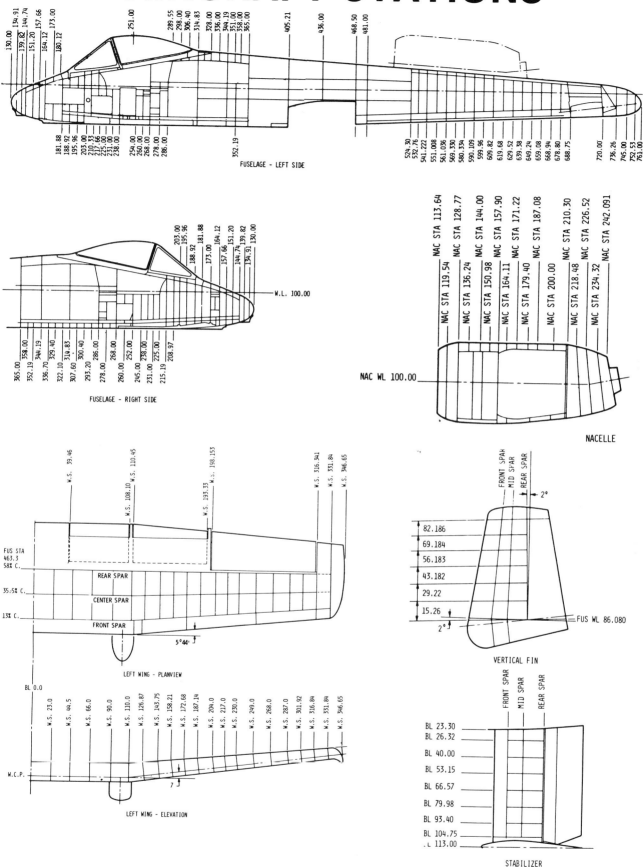

The zero reference for the fuselage stations is a point 130.00 inches forward of the nose (excluding the gun muzzle). Vertical fuselage stations are determined by waterlines. Wing stations are measured from the centerline of the fuselage, which is considered wing station zero.

THE GUN

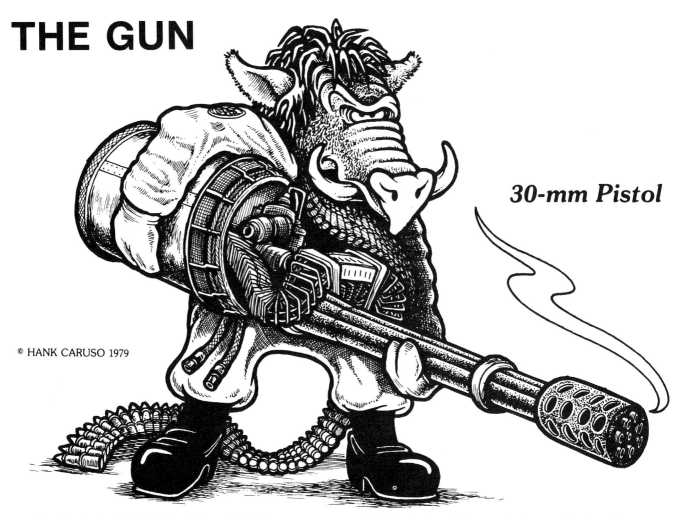

© HANK CARUSO 1979

30-mm Pistol

A major design factor in the Air Force's initial concept of the A-X CAS aircraft was a new 30mm cannon with greater tank-killing power than the existing 20mm M61A Gatling gun. In November 1970, six months after the RFP on the A-X, the Air Force asked for proposals on a new 30mm gun to be known as the GAU-8 "Avenger". The following June, General Electric and Philco-Ford were issued competitive contracts to develop the GAU-8 and four types of ammunition, while Hughes Tool Company was contracted to develop the GAU-9, a license-built version of the Swiss Oerlikon 304RF-30, as a backup system. The result of prototype testing was the June 1973 production contract awarded to General Electric.

Properly speaking, the GAU-8 is only the 'gun' part of the weapon system. The addition of the ammo feed and storage system, drive assembly, and electronic control unit (ECU) yields a weapon designated the A/A49E-6 30mm gun system. For the most part, we will follow the common practice of applying 'GAU-8' to the entire weapon.

With a full load of 1,350 armor piercing rounds, the gun, its mount, drive, and controls weigh 4,191 pounds! A linkless ammunition system helps limit the total weight, and empty shell casings are returned to the ammo drum after firing to help maintain the aircraft's center of gravity. Helixes installed in the ammo drums of some GAU-8s limit their capacities to 1174 rounds. Dual hydraulic motors drive the gun at a rate of 4,200 rounds per minute, or half that rate on one motor. The pilot's gun rate switch is in the upper right of the armament control panel (see page 14).

Within the first half second of squeezing the trigger, the GAU-8 is firing at full speed; in one second, fifty rounds are headed for the target, with seventy more per second after that. At full rate of fire, the preferred sequence is ten two-second bursts (each with a one minute gun-cooling period) but continuous 750-round bursts have been fired without barrel damage.

Four types of ammunition were developed for the GAU-8, although one, the semi-armor piercing high explosive (SAPHE) round, was not purchased. High explosive incendiary (HEI) and target practice (TP) rounds are generally similar to other cannon ammunition, although both use plastic (rather than copper) rotating bands to reduce barrel wear. Cartridge cases are made of inexpensive, lightweight aluminum. The armor piercing incendiary round (API) uses a high-density depleted uranium (DU) spike at its core. Although the Soviet press has denounced the API as an atomic weapon, DU is employed for its mass, not for its negligible radioactivity. The total kinetic energy of the round is focused at the point of the spike, giving a single round enough power to shatter the integrity of any armor skin.

The GAU-8 is internally mounted to the left of the A-10's centerline, with counterweights lining the nose wheel well to stabilize the off-center mass. The gun is depressed two degrees in its mounting to improve attack angles in a strafing run. By firing the active barrel directly along the centerline, the recoil force (averaging 10,000 pounds) does not force the A-10's nose off target.

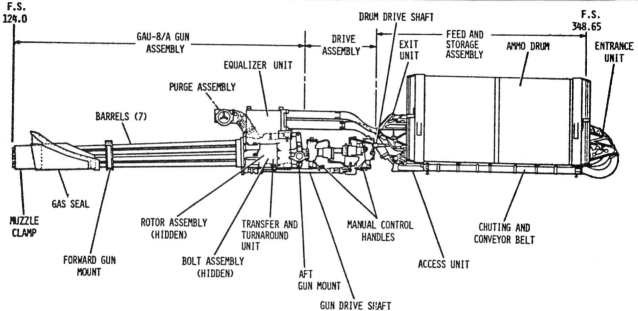

F.S. 124.0

GAU-8/A GUN ASSEMBLY

DRUM DRIVE SHAFT

DRIVE ASSEMBLY

EXIT UNIT

FEED AND STORAGE ASSEMBLY

AMMO DRUM

F.S. 348.65

ENTRANCE UNIT

EQUALIZER UNIT

PURGE ASSEMBLY

BARRELS (7)

GAS SEAL

MUZZLE CLAMP

FORWARD GUN MOUNT

ROTOR ASSEMBLY (HIDDEN)

TRANSFER AND TURNAROUND UNIT

BOLT ASSEMBLY (HIDDEN)

AFT GUN MOUNT

GUN DRIVE SHAFT

MANUAL CONTROL HANDLES

ACCESS UNIT

CHUTING AND CONVEYOR BELT

(Above) The entire A/A49E-6 gun system, with an Air Force schematic of its major components. (Fairchild Republic)

(Below) Four large panels provide unrestricted access to the gun and its subsystems. (Fairchild Republic)

The Avenger gun system in place on a preproduction airframe. *(Fairchild Republic)*

On aircraft 81-981 and subsequent, the ammo loading door
was modified by the addition of a rearward facing air scoop.

Head-on view of an early production aircraft, with access
panels buttoned up. The irregular black fairing ahead of the
nose wheel door is the ALR-46 radar warning antenna.
(Fairchild Republic)

GAU-8 in 73-1666, the third preproduction airframe. The two rows of five slots on the fuselage side vent gun gasses through
the ammo loading door. A large circular vent ahead of the loading door is for an internal gun gas purge fan.
(Fairchild Republic)

GAU-8 muzzle in one of the final production airframes. Above the gun, the bug-eyed nodes of the ALR-69 radar warning system have replaced the single black lump of earlier systems.

In an effort to keep smoke away from the engines and windscreen, A-10s are being refitted with welded gun gas diverters.

The attachment turns with the firing GAU-8, but has no independently-moving parts. Note the exposed gun barrels.

CHAFF/FLARE DISPENSING SYSTEM

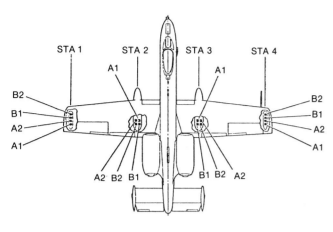

VIEW LOOKING DOWN

STORES	RELEASE SEQUENCE (STATIONS)
RR-170 A/AL CHAFF CARTRIDGES (SINGLE)	1, 4, 2, 3
RR-170 A/AL CHAFF CARTRIDGES (DOUBLE)	1 AND 4, 2 AND 3
M-206 FLARE CARTRIDGES	3, 2, 4, 1
NOTE EACH STATION WILL RELEASE ITS STORES IN THE ORDER A1, A2, B1, B2.	

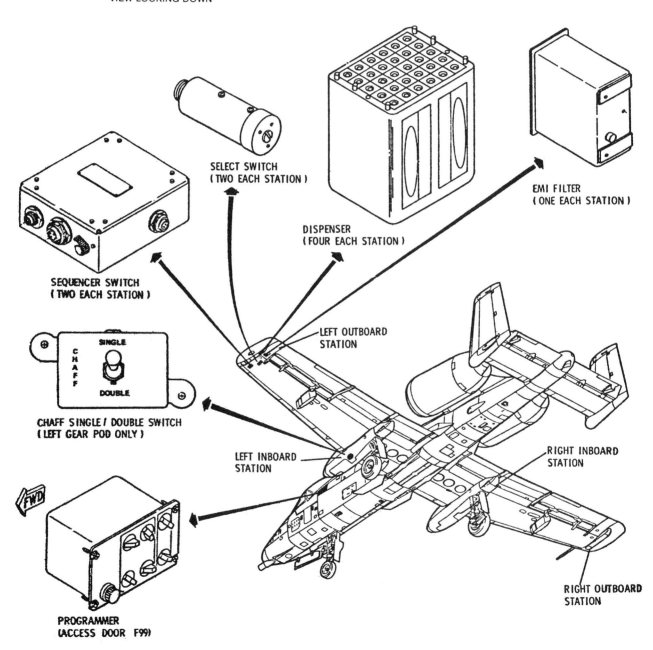

SELECT SWITCH (TWO EACH STATION)

DISPENSER (FOUR EACH STATION)

EMI FILTER (ONE EACH STATION)

SEQUENCER SWITCH (TWO EACH STATION)

CHAFF SINGLE / DOUBLE SWITCH (LEFT GEAR POD ONLY)

PROGRAMMER (ACCESS DOOR F99)

LEFT OUTBOARD STATION

LEFT INBOARD STATION

RIGHT INBOARD STATION

RIGHT OUTBOARD STATION

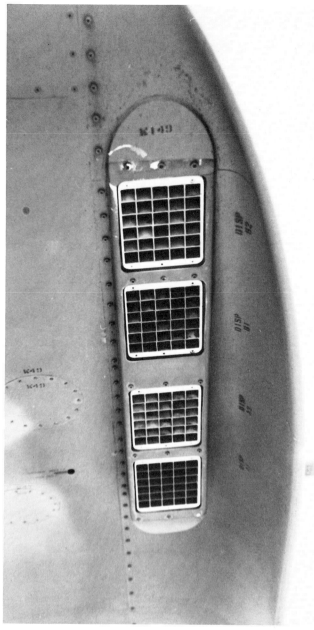

Right wing tip chaff/flare dispenser with cover in place.

As a counter-measure to ground radar stations, heat seeking (infrared), and radar guided missiles, the A-10 is equipped to dispense flares and chaff. All aircraft can carry external ALE-40 dispensers on wing racks; aircraft 77-227 and up also mount sixteen internal ALE-40(V) dispensers, with four each at the wing tips and the aft ends of the main landing gear pods. To fit the chaff/flare cartridges, the wheel sponsons were deepened and the wing tip turn-downs were thinned. The unloaded dispensers can be covered with sheet metal panels, but the panels must be removed on the ground before loading or operations.

(Left) Station #1 dispensers under the left wing tip.
(Van Winkle)

(Lower left) The original landing gear sponson ended in a tapered fairing which was undercut to clear the flaps.
(Marshall)

(Below) The fairings on serials 77-227 and subsequent were redesigned to fit four chaff/flare dispensing units.
(Van Winkle)

EXTERNAL STORES
AERONAUTICAL UNIT DESIGNATIONS

BLU-99A (T-1)/B (XI-2)

Item Identification
'U' For Unit
Serial Number
Model
Trainer-Dummy
Installation
Developmental Item

Most discussions of external stores rapidly dissolve into an alphabet soup of KMUs, LGBs, and BLUs, so a few notes explaining military aeronautical unit designations seem in order. As seen above, the code system can be rather complex, but we can generally concern ourselves with only the first three letters and the digits following the hyphen. (It is important not to confuse aeronautical unit designations with common abbreviations or MK-numbers, which will be discussed below.) Using the chart at the bottom of the page, the initial item identification letters become easily understandable: "GAU" identifies an aircraft gun; "GBU" denotes a guided bomb (irrespective of the type of guidance); a "LAU" is an aircraft-installed launcher, and on down the list.

Many weapons are composites of smaller components. A CBU cluster bomb is usually comprised of BLU bomblets inside an SUU dispenser and armed by an FMU fuse. The final designation depends on the combination of the components or submunitions - a standard SUU-30 canister becomes a CBU-52, CBU-58, or CBU-71 cluster bomb, depending on the bomblets inside.

Iron bombs are usually grouped by general weight classification under a series of "Mark" or "MK" headings rather than by aeronautical unit designations. These conventional bomb headings defy conventional logic, since a MK 82 weighs in at about 500 pounds, a MK 84 is classed at 2,000 pounds, and a MK 117 is back down around 750 pounds. Each free-fall bomb can be modified with a guidance head and fin kit: a 2000 pound (MK 84) with a KMU-353 electro-optical guidance kit becomes a GBU-8 (one of the "HoBos" or HOming BOmbs). The same iron bomb with a KMU-351

laser guidance kit becomes the GBU-10 (one of the standard "LGBs" as laser-guided bombs are abbreviated). Thus, a 2,000 pound LGB and the GBU-10 can be different descriptions of the same weapon.

Guided missiles fall under a separate designation system. The primary missile used on the A-10 is the AGM-65 Maverick, a guided air-to-ground missile (AGM). The AGM-65A is laser-guided, the AGM-65B is TV-guided (scene magnification, usually with "SCENE MAG" stenciled on the side), and the AGM-65D has imaging infrared capabilities (IIR). The training version of the Maverick, the TGM-65 or A/A37A-T6A, has no motor and no guidance fins. Six Mavericks can be carried, three each on two LAU-88 launchers at wing stations 3 and 9.

The AIM-9L Sidewinder is an infrared seeking air interception missile (AIM) which has been fitted to the A-10 with some success. The AIM-9L, nicknamed the "Lima", can track and attack an aircraft head on. This ability to "shoot 'em in the nose" has brought the added nickname of "Nosewinder". First tested by the NY-ANG in December 1981, the concept was further evaluated by the 422d TES in 1983. A dual LAU-114 launcher is attached to one of the two outboard wing stations at a combined hardware and manhour cost under $2,000 per airframe. The added sting will help Hog drivers cover themselves if bounced by an enemy, but it will be a long time before we see our first A-10 ace.

Other external stores include electronic countermeasures pods, which are designated under the AN/ALQ (or simply ALQ) series. To clear open speed brakes, the A-10 generally mounts its ALQ-119 or ALQ-131 far forward on an outboard rack.

Aeronautical Item Identification Designators

BB	EXPLOSIVE ITEMS	CN	MISCELLANEOUS CONTAINERS
BD	SIMULATED BOMBS	DS	TARGET DETECTING DEVICES
BL	BOMBS & MINES	FM	MUNITIONS FUZES
BR	BOMB RACKS & SHACKLES	FS	MUNITIONS FUZE SAFETY-ARMING DEVICE
BS	MUNITION STABILIZING & RETARDING DEVICES	FZ	FUZE-RELATED ITEMS
CB	END ITEM CLUSTER BOMBS	GA	AIRCRAFT GUN
CC	ACTUATOR CARTRIDGES	GB	GUIDED BOMBS
CD	CLUSTERED MUNITIONS (NOT END ITEMS)	GF	GUN-RELATED ITEMS
		GP	PODDED GUNS

GU	MISCELLANEOUS GUNS	PA	MUNITIONS DISPENSING DEVICES, EXTERNAL
KA	MUNITIONS CLUSTERING HARDWARE	PD	LEAFLET DISPENSER
KM	KITS	PG	AMMUNITION
LA	AIRCRAFT INSTALLED LAUNCHERS	PW	INTERNAL DISPENSERS
LK	AMMUNITION LINKS	RD	DUMMY ROCKETS
LM	GROUND BASED LAUNCHERS	RL	ROCKETS
LU	ILLUMINATION UNITS	SA	GUN-BOMB-ROCKET SIGHTS
MA	MISCELLANEOUS ARMAMENT ITEMS	SU	STORES SUSPENSION & RELEASE ITEMS
MD	MISCELLANEOUS SIMULATED MUNITIONS	TM	MISCELLANEOUS TANKS
MH	MUNITIONS HANDLING EQUIPMENT	TT	TEST ITEMS
MJ	MUNITIONS COUNTERMEASURES	WD	WARHEADS
ML	MISCELLANEOUS MUNITIONS	WT	TRAINING WARHEADS
MT	MOUNTS		

NORMAL STORES RELEASE SEQUENCE WITH TERS

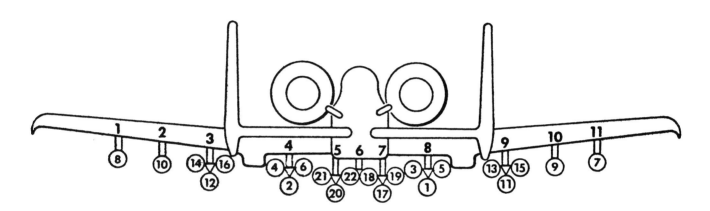

REAR VIEW

External stores are suspended from a series of wing stations numbered from 1 (at the left wing tip) to 11 (at the right). Stations 1, 2, 10, and 11 are MAU-50 racks and carry one store each (unless Sidewinders are mounted). Stations 1 and 11 also house external actuators for the ailerons. Stations 3 through 9 are MAU-40 racks and carry single stores or TERS capable of carrying three bombs each. During operational testing, stations 5, 6, and 7 mounted multiple ejector racks (MERs) capable of carrying six bombs each, but this rack was never certified for the A-10 and is not authorized for use.

Since stores cannot be carried on all three under-fuselage stations at once, #6 is often removed to cut down on drag. Some units are also removing the racks from stations 5 and 7, and most A-10s seen today fly without racks on stations 2 and 10.

One other removeable pylon is the Pave Penny mount on the right side of the forward fuselage. This position is dedicated, and no other stores may be mounted there.

Plastic models of the A-10 come with a staggering array of weapons options, but using all that plastic will usually result in a model of an aircraft that shouldn't be able to taxi to the runway. Modelers have the same options for hanging bombs beneath their A-10s as Air Force armorers do. The charts on pages 58 through 61 are refined from official documents and show the approved maximum stores loads for the Hog. Mirror images are authorized, and partial configurations can be accomplished using the following ground rules:

1) Stores may be deleted in their normal release sequence.

2) All stores on station 6, or on stations 5 and 7, or on stations 1 and 11 may be deleted out of sequence.

3) With BDU-33s mounted, stations 9 and 3 may be deleted prior to stations 8 and 4.

4) With mixed weapons types, any type of weapon may be deleted independently of any other type.

By manipulating the rules and the stores charts it is possible to create many more legal store configurations for operational aircraft. But please, modelers, no matter how threatening it would look, don't start gluing spare Phoenix missiles to your wing racks!

EXTERNAL STORES LOADING CONFIGURATIONS

Left Table

STORE TYPE	LINE NUMBER	1	2	3	4	5	6	7	8	9	10	11	QUANTITY	NOTES
Mk-82 LDGP/ Snakeye or Mk-36 or Mk-20 Cluster or SUU-30 Dispenser	1	●	●	●	●	●		●	●	●	●	●	10	
	2	●	●	▼(TER)	●	●		●	▼(TER)	●	●		14	
	3	●	●	▼(TER)	▼(TER)	●		●	▼(TER)	▼(TER)	●		18	
GBU-8	4			●	●				●	●			4	
GBU-10	5			●	●				●	●			4	
GBU-12	6	●		●	●				●	●	●		6	
AGM-65 Missile	7			▼(TER)					▼(TER)				6	
	8			▼					▼				4	
	9			▼					▼				2	
				▼					▼					
				▼					▼					
				▼					▼					

STORE TYPE	LINE NUMBER	1	2	3	4	5	6	7	8	9	10	11	QUANTITY	NOTES
SUU-20 Pract. Dispenser / Mk-82 LDGP/Snakeye	1	82	82	82	20	20		20	20	82	82	82	4(SUU) 6(Mk)	
SUU-20 Pract. Dispenser / Mk-84 LDGP	2			84	20	20		20	20	84			4(SUU) 2(Mk)	
SUU-20 Pract. Dispenser / GBU-12	3	12		12	20	20		20	20	12		12	4(SUU) 4(GBU)	
SUU-20 Pract. Dispenser / GBU-10	4			10	20	20		20	20	10			4(SUU) 2(GBU)	
SUU-20 Pract. Dispenser / GBU-8	5			8	20	20		20	20	8			4(SUU) 2(GBU)	
SUU-20 Pract. Dispenser / LAU-68 Rocket Launcher	6		68	68	20	20		20	20	68	68		4(SUU) 4(LAU)	
BDU-33 Pract. Bomb / Mk-82 LDGP/Snakeye	1	82	82	33	33	82		82	33	33	82	82	12(BDU) 6(Mk)	
BDU-33 Pract. Bomb / Mk-84 LDGP	2			33	33	84		84	33	33			12(BDU) 2(Mk)	

Right Table

STORE TYPE	LINE NUMBER	1	2	3	4	5	6	7	8	9	10	11	QUANTITY	NOTES
Mk-84 LDGP	10			●	●				●	●			4	
	11			●	●	●			●	●	●		6	
BLU-52	12	●	●	●	●	●			●	●	●	●	8	
SUU-25 Flare Dispenser	13		●								●		2	
	14		●	●						●	●		4	
	15		●	▼(TER)						▼(TER)	●		8	
SUU-20 Pract. Dispenser	16				●	●		●	●				4	
SUU-23 Gun Pod	17				●				●				2	

STORE TYPE	LINE NUMBER	1	2	3	4	5	6	7	8	9	10	11	QUANTITY	NOTES
SUU-20 Pract. Dispenser / Mk-20 Cluster	7	Mk	Mk	Mk	SUU	SUU		SUU	SUU	Mk	Mk	Mk	4(SUU) 6(Mk)	
SUU-20 Pract. Dispenser / SUU-30 Dispenser	8	30	30	30	20	20		20	20	30	30	30	4(SUU) 6(SUU-30)	
SUU-20 Pract. Dispenser / AGM-65 Missile	9			65(TER)	20	20		20	20	65(TER)			4(SUU) 4(AGM)	
SUU-20 Pract. Dispenser / BDU-33 Pract. Bomb	10			33(TER)	33(TER)	20		20	33(TER)	33(TER)			2(SUU) 12(BDU)	
SUU-20 Pract. Dispenser / SUU-25 Flare Dispenser	11		25	25	20	20		20	20	25	25		4(SUU) 4(SUU-25)	
BDU-33 Pract. Bomb / LAU-68 Rocket Launcher	7		68	33(TER)	33(TER)	33(TER)		33(TER)	33(TER)	33(TER)	68		18(BDU) 2(LAU)	
BDU-33 Pract. Bomb / Mk-20 Cluster	8	20	20	33(TER)	33(TER)	20		20	33(TER)	33(TER)	20	20	12(BDU) 6(Mk)	

Aircraft stores loading and suspension chart (stations 1–11). Triangle symbols indicate multiple-carriage (TER) racks.

Left Table

Store Type	Line No.	1	2	3	4	5	6	7	8	9	10	11	Quantity
Mk-20 Cluster	1	20	25	20	20	20		20	20	20	25	20	8 (Mk) / 2 (SUU)
SUU-25 Flare Dispenser	2	20	20	25	20	20		20	20	25	20	20	8 (Mk) / 6 (SUU)
	3	20	25	25	20	20		20	20	20	25	20	12 (Mk) / 2 (SUU)
	4	20	25	20	20	20		20	20	20	25	20	14 (Mk) / 2 (SUU)
	5	20	20	25	20	20		20	20	25	20	20	12 (Mk) / 6 (SUU)
MK-20 Cluster	6	20	68	68	20	20		20	20	68	68	20	6 (Mk) / 4 (LAU)
LAU-68 Rocket Launcher	7	20	20	68	20	20		20	20	68	20	20	8 (Mk) / 6 (LAU)
	8	20	68	20	20	20		20	20	20	68	20	12 (Mk) / 2 (LAU)
	9	20	68	20	20	20		20	20	20	68	20	14 (Mk) / 2 (LAU)
	10	20	20	68	68	20		20	68	68	20	20	6 (Mk) / 12 (LAU)
	11	20	20	20	68	20		20	68	20	20	20	12 (Mk) / 6 (LAU)
Mk-20 Cluster	7	20	20	82	82	82		82	82	82	20	20	4 (Mk) / 6 (Mk-82)
Mk-82 LDGP/Snakeye	8	20	20	20	82	82		82	82	20	20	20	10 (Mk) / 4 (Mk-82)
	9	82	82	82	20	20		20	20	82	82	82	4 (Mk) / 10 (Mk-82)
	10	20	82	82	82	20		20	82	82	82	20	4 (Mk) / 14 (Mk-82)
	11	82	20	20	20	82		82	20	20	20	82	14 (Mk) / 4 (Mk-82)
BDU-33 Pract. Bomb	1			▲	▲	▲		▲	▲	▲			18
	2			▲	▲	▲		▲	▲	▲			12
LAU-68 Rocket Launcher	3		●	●	●			●	●	●			6
	4		●	▲	●			●	▲	●			10
	5			▲	▲			▲	▲				14
GBU-8	13	12		8	8				8	8		12	4 (GBU) / 2 (GBU-12)
GBU-12	14	12		12	8				8	12		12	2 (GBU) / 4 (GBU-12)
GBU-8 / GBU-10	15			10	8				8	10			2 (GBU) / 2 (GBU-10)
Mk-84 LDGP / Mk-82 LDGP/Snakeye	3	82	82	82	84	84		84	84	82	82	82	4 (Mk) / 6 (Mk-82)
	4	82	82	82	84	84		84	84	82	82	82	4 (Mk) / 10 (Mk-82)

Right Table

Store Type	Line No.	1	2	3	4	5	6	7	8	9	10	11	Quantity
LAU-68 Rocket Launcher	12	82	68	68	82	82		82	82	68	68	82	4 (LAU) / 6 (Mk)
Mk-82 LDGP/Snakeye	13	82	82	68	82	82		82	82	68	82	82	6 (LAU) / 8 (Mk)
	14	82	68	82	82	82		82	82	82	68	82	2 (LAU) / 12 (Mk)
	15	82	68	82	82	82		82	82	82	68	82	2 (LAU) / 14 (Mk)
	16	82	82	68	68	82		82	68	68	82	82	12 (LAU) / 6 (Mk)
	17	82	82	82	68	82		82	68	82	82	82	6 (LAU) / 12 (Mk)
LAU-68 Rocket Launcher / GBU-12	18	12	68	12	12			12	12	68	12		2 (LAU) / 6 (GBU)
	19	12	68	68	12			12	68	68	12		4 (LAU) / 4 (GBU)
	20	12	68	68	12			12	68	68	12		8 (LAU) / 4 (GBU)
SUU-30 Dispenser / Mk-20 Cluster	1	20	20	30	30	30		30	30	30	20	20	6 (SUU) / 4 (Mk)
	2	20	20	20	30	30		30	30	20	20	20	4 (SUU) / 10 (Mk)
	3	20	30	30	30	20		20	30	30	30	20	14 (SUU) / 4 (Mk)
	4	30	20	20	20	30		30	20	20	20	30	4 (SUU) / 14 (Mk)
	5	30	30	20	30	20		20	30	20	30	30	10 (SUU) / 8 (Mk)
	6	30	30	30	20	20		20	20	30	30	30	10 (SUU) / 4 (Mk)
600 Gallon Fuel Tank	6			●		●		●					3
MXU-648 Cargo Pod	7					●							1
ALQ-119 or -131(V) ECM Pod	8	●									●		2
BL-755 Cluster Weapon	9	●	●	●	●	●		●	●	●	●		10
SUU-25 Flare Dispenser / GBU-10	11		25	10	10			10	10	25			2 (SUU) / 4 (GBU)
GBU-8 / Mk-82 LDGP/SELD/SEHD	12	82	82	8	8	82		82	8	8	82	82	4 (GBU) / 6 (Mk)
GBU-10 / Mk-82 LDGP/SELD/SEHD	16	82	82	10	10	82		82	10	10	82	82	4 (GBU) / 6 (Mk)
GBU-10 / GBU-12	1	12		10	10			10	10		12		4 (GBU) / 2 (GBU-12)
	2	12		12	10			10	12		12		2 (GBU) / 4 (GBU-12)

Left Table

STORE TYPE	LINE NUMBER	1	2	3	4	5	6	7	8	9	10	11	QUANTITY	NOTES
AGM-65 Missile	1	82	82	65	82	82		82	82	65	82	82	6(AGM) 8(Mk)	
Mk-82 LDGP/Snakeye	2	82	82	65	82	82		82	82	65	82	82	6(AGM) 12(Mk)	
AGM-65 Missile / Mk-84 LDGP	3			65	84	84		84	84	65			6(AGM) 4(Mk)	
AGM-65 Missile / GBU-12	4		12	65		12		12		65		12	6(AGM) 4(GBU)	
AGM-65 Missile / GBU-10	5			65		10		10		65			6(AGM) 2(GBU)	
AGM-65 Missile / GBU-8	6			65		8		8		65			6(AGM) 2(GBU)	
SUU-30 Dispenser	1	30	30	82	82	82		82	82	82	30	30	4(SUU) 6(Mk)	
Mk-82 LDGP/Snakeye	2	30	30	30	82	82		82	82	30	30	30	10(SUU) 4(Mk)	
	3	82	82	82	30	30		30	30	82	82	82	4(SUU) 10(Mk)	
	4	30	82	82	82	30		30	82	82	82	30	4(SUU) 14(Mk)	
	5	82	30	30	30	82		82	30	30	30	82	14(SUU) 4(Mk)	
	6	82	30	82	30	82		82	30	82	30	82	8(SUU) 10(Mk)	
SUU-30 Dispenser / MK-84 LDGP	7	30	30	30	84	84		84	84	30	30	30	6(SUU) 4(Mk)	
	8	30	30	30	84	84		84	84	30	30	30	10(SUU) 4(Mk)	
SUU-30 Dispenser / GBU-8	9	30	30	8	8			30	8	8	30	30	6(SUU) 4(GBU)	
BDU-33 Pract. Bomb / GBU-12	3	12		33	33	33		33	33	33		12	18(BDU) 2(GBU)	
BDU-33 Pract. Bomb / GBU-10	4			33	10	33		33	10	33			12(BDU) 2(GBU)	
BDU-33 Pract. Bomb / GBU-8	5			33	8	33		33	8	33			12(BDU) 2(GBU)	
BDU-33 Pract. Bomb / SUU-25 Flare Dispenser	6		25	33	33	33		33	33	33	25		18(BDU) 2(SUU)	
Mk-20 Cluster / GBU-10	15	20	20	10	10	20		20	10	10	20	20	6(Mk) 4(GBU)	
Mk-20 Cluster / GBU-8	16	20	20	8	8	20		20	8	8	20	20	6(Mk) 4(GBU)	

Right Table

STORE TYPE	LINE NUMBER	1	2	3	4	5	6	7	8	9	10	11	QUANTITY	NOTES
AGM-65 Missile	7		68	65	68				68	65	68		6(AGM) 4(LAU)	
LAU-68 Rocket Launcher	8		68	65	68				68	65	68		6(AGM) 8(LAU)	
AGM-65 Missile	9	20	20	65	20	20		20	20	65	20	20	6(AGM) 8(AGM)	
Mk-20 Cluster	10	20	20	65	20	20		20	20	65	20	20	6(AGM) 12(Mk)	
AGM-65 Missile	11	30	30	65	30	30		30	30	65	30	30	6(AGM) 8(SUU)	
SUU-30 Dispenser	12	30	30	65	30	30		30	30	65	30	30	12(SUU) 6(AGM)	
AGM-65 Missile / SUU-25 Flare Dispenser	13		25	65					65	25			6(AGM) 2(SUU)	
SUU-30 Dispenser / GBU-10	10	30	30	10	10	30		30	10	10	30	30	6(SUU) 4(GBU)	
SUU-30 Dispenser / LAU-68 Rocket Launcher	11	30	68	68	30	30		30	30	68	68	30	6(SUU) 4(LAU)	
	12	30	30	68	30	30		30	30	68	30	30	8(SUU) 6(LAU)	
	13	30	68	30	30			30	30	30	68	30	12(SUU) 2(LAU)	
	14	30	68	30	30			30	30	30	68	30	14(SUU) 2(LAU)	
	15	30	68	68	30			30	68	68	30		6(SUU) 12(LAU)	
	16	30	30	68	30	30		30	68	30	30		12(SUU) 6(LAU)	
SUU-30 Dispenser	17	30	25	30	30			30	30	30	25	30	8(SUU) 2(SUU-25)	
SUU-25 Dispenser	18	30	30	25	30			30	30	25	30	30	8(SUU) 6(SUU-25)	
	19	30	25	30	30			30	30	30	25	30	12(SUU) 2(SUU-25)	
BDU-33 Pract. Bomb / SUU-30 Dispenser	9	30	30	33	33	30		30	33	33	30	30	12(BDU) 6(SUU)	
BDU-33 Pract. Bomb / AGM-65 Missile	10		65	33	33			33	33	65			12(BDU) 4(AGM)	
BDU-33 Pract. Bomb / LAU-68 Rocket Launcher	11		25	68	33	33		33	33	68	25		12(BDU) 2(LAU) 2(SUU)	
SUU-25 Flare Dispenser	12		25	68	33	33		33	33	68	25		12(BDU) 6(LAU) 2(SUU)	
Mk-20 Cluster / Mk-82 LDGP/Snakeye	12	82	82	20	82	20		20	82	20	82	82	8(Mk) 10(Mk-82)	
Mk-20 Cluster / Mk-84 LDGP	13	20	20	20	84	84		84	84	20	20	20	6(Mk) 4(Mk-84)	
	14	20	20	20	84	84		84	84	20	20	20	10(Mk) 4(Mk-84)	

STATION LOADING AND SUSPENSION

	1	2	3	4	5	6	7	8	9	10	11
LAU-68 ROCKET		25	68	68				68	68	25	
SUU-25 FLARE DISPENSER		25	68	68				68	68	25	
		68	25	68				68	25	68	
		25	68	68				68	68	25	
SUU-25 FLARE DISPENSER / MK-82 LDGP SNAKEYE	82	25	82	82	82		82	82	82	25	82
	82	82	25	82	82		82	82	25	82	82
	82	25	82	82	82		82	82	82	25	82
	82	25	82	82	82		82	82	82	25	82
	82	82	25	82	82		82	82	25	82	82
SUU-25 FLARE DISPENSER / MK-84 LDGP		25	84	84	84		84	84	84	25	
MXU-648			FUEL		FUEL	648					
			648		FUEL	FUEL					
600 GAL FUEL TANK			FUEL		648	FUEL					
		648	FUEL		648	FUEL	648				

STATION LOADING AND SUSPENSION

	1	2	3	4	5	6	7	8	9	10	11
GBU-12 MK-82 LDGP			12						82		
MK-82 GP & ALQ-119	ALQ		MK	MK		MK		MK	MK		MK
SUU-30 & ALQ-119	ALQ		SUU	SUU		SUU		SUU	SUU		SUU
MK-82 & AGM-65			65	82				82			
MXU-648 & AGM-65			65	MXU		MXU		MXU			
LAU-68 BDU-33 & TGM-65		68		33	33		33	33	65		
SUU-25 BDU-33 & TGM-65			65	33	33		33	33	25		
MXU-648 600 GAL FUEL TANK & AGM-65			65	MXU		FUEL		MXU			
			65	FUEL		MXU		FUEL			
ALQ-119 600 GAL FUEL TANK & MK-82	ALQ	82	82	82		FUEL		82	82	82	
LAU-68 MK-84 & SUU-25		25	68		84		84		68	25	
ALQ-119 or ALQ-131 AGM-65 600 GAL FUEL TANK MXU-648	ALQ		65	FUEL		MXU		FUEL	65		
	ALQ		65	FUEL		MXU		FUEL			
	ALQ			FUEL		MXU		FUEL	65		
ALQ-119 or ALQ-131 TER-9 600 GAL FUEL TANK MXU-648	ALQ		TER	FUEL		MXU		FUEL	TER		
ALQ-119 LAU-88 600 GAL FUEL TANK	ALQ		LAU			FUEL			LAU		

This is a live MK 82 500 pound bomb on station 8. The band on the nose is yellow. Note the fuse in the nose and the arming wire.　(Kinzey)

Close-up detail of a MK 20 Rockeye anti-tank cluster bomb on station 4. This is a training version of the Rockeye.　(Kinzey)

Preproduction airframe 76-668 during ordinance tests at Edwards. MK 20 Rockeye cluster bombs are mounted on racks 4, 5, 7, and 8, and live Mavericks are on LAU-88 rails at stations 3 and 9. Station 6 has been removed. (Van Winkle)

Small blue BDU-33 practice bombs hang from a TER-9.

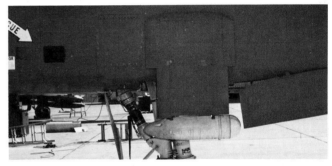

Pave Penny, the AN/AAS-35 passive laser seeker on a pre-production airframe in 1975. (USAF)

The luggage rack, officially the MXU-648 aircraft cargo pod. suspended below station #6.

What's green and dangerous? Well, it's not a frog with a hand grenade! AIM-9L's mounted at station 1 of a 422dTES Hog add a new dimension to the A-10's mission. *(422TES)*

With no motor or guidance fins, the A/A37A-T6A training version of the Maverick missile cannot be launched. It provides the pilot with TV images for simulated missile runs. Note the unusual single rail mount.

The A-10's 600 gallon external tanks are the same models carried by F-111's. Here a spotted Warthog prepares for a ferry flight to Germany for Exercise Coronet Jay in January 1978. *(USAF)*

TF-34 ENGINE

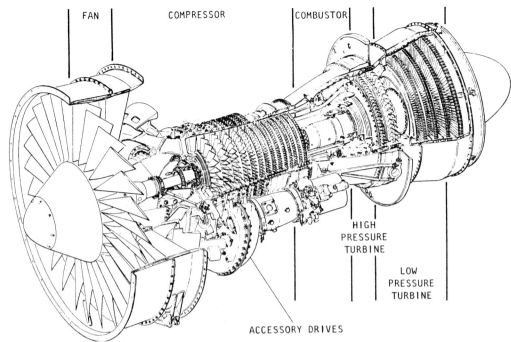

FAN COMPRESSOR COMBUSTOR HIGH PRESSURE TURBINE LOW PRESSURE TURBINE ACCESSORY DRIVES

Left side of a TF34-GE-100 engine. The TF34 can be mounted in either nacelle without modification.

Right side of the same engine, with mounting pylon on top. The engine is secured to the aircraft with only four bolts.

Remove the right engine, lie on the floor, and this is what you'll see. Two cables hang from an external hoist atop the nacelle to lift a new engine into position.

Tail end view of the left engine. 85% of the A-10's thrust comes from cold fan air which bypasses the combustion chamber.

MODELER'S SECTION

PRODUCT REVIEW POLICY.*In each of our publications we will try to review kits and decals that are available to the scale modeler. We hope to be able to review every currently available kit that is useable by the scale modeler. Kits produced in the past that are no longer generally available, and those more intended to be toys than accurate scale models will not usually be covered. Additionally, we do not intend to give a complete step-by-step correction-by-correction account of how to build each kit. Instead we intend to give a brief description of what is available to the modeler, and point out some of the good and not-so-good points of each kit or product. In this way we hope to give an overall picture of what the modeler has readily available for his use in building the particular aircraft involved.*

KIT REVIEWS

GENERAL COMMENTS

Modelers can choose from A-10 kits by nine manufacturers in four scales with varying degrees of detail and authenticity. With the exception of Matchbox's YA-10, all the models represent A-10As. The two-seater never caught on with the military, and never caught on with the kit designers either. All of the kits are 1/48th scale or smaller, which seems rather a shame. A 1/32nd scale kit (twenty-inch wing span) would offer modelers incredible room for detailing.

There are two problems common to all the kits, so rather than repeat them in each review, they are covered here. Thinking that the A-10 is like most normal airplanes, model manufacturers have given their kits' wings straight trailing edges from the fuselage past the ailerons. In truth, the ailerons have fixed trim tabs which are always pitched up, out of line with the rest of the wing, and moveable trim tabs which are rarely in line. Second, the A-10's rear fuselage is heavily riveted - no stove bolts, but lots of rounded heads. No kit really approximates this effect, and few modelers are self-destructive enough to attempt the job either.

1/144th SCALE KIT

LS Kit Numbers A-207 and A-208

The littlest A-10 is also one of the nicest. Obviously, one won't find the detail of a 1/48th scale Tamiya kit here, but the forms and shapes of the Warthog are well executed in

LS 1/144th scale A-10 built by Jim Galloway.   (Kinzey)

sixty-one finely-scribed parts. Most of the antenna are correctly represented, a major feat in this scale! A little detail work in the cockpit, a light sanding of the wing tip turndowns, and it is ready for paint. Stores include three fuel tanks, six Mavericks, two Rockeyes, six 2,000 lb. bombs, an ALQ-119, and an ALE-40 chaff/flare pod.

Kit 207 is molded in white, while 208 is in green. Otherwise the decals are the only difference. (See decal summary below.) We recommend this kit.

1/100th SCALE KIT

Takara Kit Number 10

Wait 'till Theron Rinehart hears about this! Just when his company thinks the foreign market won't buy A-10s, the Royal Aslan Air Force starts flying them. The kit even comes with a 1/24th scale figure of pilot Greg Gaiz, evidently one of the heros of some Japanese adventure cartoon. Perhaps this is what AstroBoy would have flown if he had only stuck around!

The cartoon may help sell the kit in Japan, but this model is good enough to stand on its own merits elsewhere. The 78 olive drab parts fit together well, though care is needed when attaching the wings to ensure proper dihedral. Surface scribing is very good, though not always better than the smaller LS kit.

65

Box art for the Takara 1/100th scale kit. (Kinzey)

When mounting the stores, use only one of the ALQ-119 pods, and mount that farther forward on its rack. Also included with the kit are GBU-8 and GBU-10 smart bombs, twelve 500 lb. bombs and two MERs, a 600 gallon fuel tank, six Mavericks, and two external ALE-40 dispensers. Two ground crew figures help with dioramas, and a stand is provided for a wheels-up display.

Although this is a rather small kit in perhaps the least popular of the "standard" modeling scales, it is still quite good and we recommend it.

1/72nd SCALE KITS

Matchbox Kit Number PK-121

The Matchbox choice to present a YA-10 after the A-10A had already entered production may have been a brave attempt to represent the Warthog as no other company would. The model is depicted in the same configuration as the prototypes on rollout: no slats, no strakes, no trailing edge fairings, and no GAU-8 (the 20mm Vulcan is mounted).

But the Matchbox kit is a bear to assemble! Parts fit together poorly and require a great deal of filling and sanding. The model lacks many basic details and shows numerous inaccuracies. The prominent flap guides are gone, and the cockpit is empty except for a livingroom chair. The

The Matchbox kit in 1/72nd scale is the only model that represents the YA-10 prototypes. (Kinzey)

engine nacelles are mounted too close to the fuselage, and the wheel sponsons are the wrong shape and are poorly positioned. Fuselage scribing is minimal. The vertical tails do not agree with prototype or production design, and external stores are limited to eighteen nondescript "little bombs". The kit appears inaccurate, even at a casual glance.

Still, it *is* the only YA-10 on the market. With a tube of green stuff, a good file, and a large spare parts box, this can be turned into a YA-10 more easily than any another kit.

Airfix/MPC Kit Number 1-4407

The Airfix A-10A, like the Hasegawa kit, falls together right from the box. There's a bit more putty and sanding involved, but this is still minimal. This is a sound kit for the modeler to work with, and it's the only kit to put the flaps on the lower wing half where they can be cut out and lowered.

Airfix's detail is almost light enough to be masked by a coat of paint, which is a blessing in this case. The engraver who etched this kit's panel lines has done the sloppiest job ever seen on a model airplane. Where two lines intersect, they invariably run past each other, leaving little tails all over the surface. This is particularly ugly on the ammo loading door, with its skewed raised lines representing the gun gas vents. Those who like to rescribe their panel lines will have a hefty job with this kit.

The wing chord cross section is also a bit too curved underneath, but lowering the flaps and opening the speed brakes can help. Otherwise, flatten out the high spots of the lower surface along the wing racks. The wing slats should also be closed a little more, but at least there is the option to show them open.

The cockpit has a well-executed raised instrument panel and a reasonable ACES II, but a few added details will be helpful.

External stores include a 600 gallon fuel tank, six Mavericks, two Rockeyes, three 500 lb. low-drag bombs, one each laser-guided and electro-optical guided 2,000 pounder, and an ALQ-119. Decals are for the same 23d TFW aircraft as the Hasegawa kit. Here, the blue of the tail band is too dark, and, once again, the national insignia should all be the same size.

Monogram Kit Numbers 5405 and 5430

One of the first Hogs on the market, Monogram's A-10 depicts a preproduction or early production airframe. Since filing the flap guides, relocating the antenna, and, perhaps adding chaff/flare dispensers will yield a later version, the kit can work for almost any A-10A.

The one major complaint with this kit is its fit. Parts go together poorly and require careful filling and sanding at the wings, engine mounts, and tail. The only glaring inaccuracy is the over-long GAU-8, which should be shortened before being glued to the fuselage.

Cockpit detail is good, with a raised instrument panel

and ESCAPAC seat covered by a two-position canopy. An internal boarding ladder is provided. There is a TF34 engine to mount in the left nacelle, but the engine access doors are incorrect, and they should be rebuilt using the photos and drawings in this book as a guide. When closed, the nacelles appear a bit too egg-shaped, but some light file work can take care of this. The raised surface detail is well done, with the ailerons being particularly nice.

External stores include eighteen low-drag 500 lb. bombs with two MERs and two TERs. (Monogram's bomb racks are among the most detailed available, a definite plus on this kit or in the spare parts box!) Six laser-guided 500 pounders and a fuel tank round out the stores.

Original kit (5405) markings are for a two-toned MASK-10A gray aircraft of the 355th TFW. With exception of the black "DM", these should be replaced with 36118 gunship gray markings. Note also that the national insignia should all have the same eighteen-inch diameter stars. We recommend this kit.

Hasegawa/Minicraft Kit Number 1206

Hasegawa's production version of the A-10 is a pleasure to build - it falls together straight from the box! It is the best A-10 in this scale. You can't fault the outline and the overall feel of this kit.

Detail - what there is of it - is very good, but inconsistent. For example, the fuselage panel scribing forward of the wing is beautiful, with finely raised screws and dzus fasteners contrasted by cleanly sunken vents.

Yet, aft of the wing, the fuselage has a few raised panel lines and sunken APU vents, but no rivets at all. The square sunken 'vent' just above the wing fairing should actually be a rubber bumper to protect the fuselage when the engine access door swings down.

The cockpit includes instrument panel decals and a slightly undersized ACES II seat; the boarding ladder is included. Weapons offered are six Mavericks, twelve 500 lb. practice bombs (with two MERs), two GBU-10s, and two 2,000 lb. low-drags. Covered ALE-40(V) dispensers are mounted at the wing tips and wheel sponsons, but these could use a little work to correct their shape. And the aileron actuators are missing from racks 1 and 11.

Decals are for the HQ flight of the 23d TFW and a MASK-10A aircraft of the 355th TFW. As with the Monogram kit, the black markings for the 355th Hog should be replaced with gunship gray decals. We recommend this kit.

Hasegawa 1/72nd scale kit built by Jim Hagey, and entered in the contest at the 1985 IPMS National Convention.
(Kinzey)

Monogram 1/72nd scale kit built by Bert Kinzey. (Kinzey)

1/48th SCALE KITS

ESCI Kit Numbers 4005 and 4070

ESCI made its A-10 the most ambitious Warthog kit yet,

adding more features than any other manufacturer. And in the US kit (Scale Craft 4005), the instruction sheet offers the young modeler something not seen for years - an explanation of what he's putting together! He's told, among other things, that the decelerons open as speed brakes or move together as conventional ailerons. He's told that the bump on the tail is a light and that the pod hanging from the fuselage is a Pave Penny laser seeker (not just Part 3A). Model companies remind us that most kit sales go to younger modelers, so it's nice to see an instruction sheet that keeps that in mind. Unfortunately, when ESCI re-released this kit, this nice information was gone. Although the kit is ambitious, it falls short of its ambition. Our sample had problems holding the glue, so a good detergent wash of all the parts is in order. The fit is still going to be poor, and the overall shape of the final model will be incorrect. The rear fuselage pinches in, the engines sit too low and close to the fuselage, and the pitchdown of the wing tips is wrong.

But the kit provides an open fuselage to show the GAU-8 clear back to the ammo drum, and that alone will make it popular.

If you find yourself building this kit, do not install the nose gear until the end. Build up the inside of the fuselage before construction to keep the wheel well and cockpit from detaching themselves from the lower fuselage. It appears that ESCI also planned for a boarding ladder, but this is not included, and the closed boarding ladder door is a poor fit. There is an actuator to raise the canopy, but the canopy comes as one piece. Speed brakes can be opened, but they are totally incorrect, even splitting the moveable trim tab with the rest of the aileron.

Stores include two ALQ-119s, four 500 lb. low drag bombs, two rocket pods, two Rockeyes, twelve 500 lb. Snakeyes (on two MERs), and six Mavericks.

The model is obviously popular with younger modelers, but has less value to more experienced modelers.

Tamiya Kit Number MA-123

What a nice kit! In our estimation, this is the best model of the A-10 available in any scale.

The model represents one of the first ten A-10As, so don't forget those flap guides for later versions. The cockpit is well done, except that the instruments and consoles are decals rather than being raised on the plastic. The highly detailed landing gear builds up from several parts.

Run a file around the landing gear sponsons (which are a little too square) and the model is ready to paint.

External stores include one each electro-optical and laser-guided 2,000 lb. bomb, six Mavericks, twelve 500 lb. low drag bombs (on two MERs), two chaff/flare pods, and two ALQ-119s. The kit was produced before photos of the ALQ-119 mount was published, so remove the pod from the rack and remount it flush to the rack's trailing edge. The standard ALQ-119 mounting is only one pod. The two MERs leave a lot to be desired, but since the A-10 was never certified to carry them, simply discard these. TERs from 1/48th scale Monogram or Hasegawa kits could be used instead.

Surface scribing is delicate and nice. Be careful not to remove it when sanding. Molding of parts is crisp and clean as it is with most Tamiya kits.

Details include a two-piece canopy, boarding ladder, pilot figure, optional position landing gear doors, and nice decals with several choices. (See the decal summary below.) However, one error in the decals should be noted. Aircraft 75-261 never wore the graded MASK 10A scheme shown in the instructions.

Although it represents one of the early A-10As, and is therefore missing the updates and improvements made to later aircraft, the Tamiya kit ranks as the best kit released to date. We recommend this kit.

Revell Kit Numbers 4503 and 4516

The Revell A-10 is also a very nice kit, second only to Tamiya's. The surface scribing is comparable, as is the overall accuracy. Revell's wheel sponsons even have a more accurate shape. The Revell cockpit offers raised instrument panels, but the Tamiya has more of the other

Tamiya's 1/48th scale A-10 rates as the best kit available of the Warthog. (Kinzey)

Revell's A-10 kit in 1/48th scale. (Revell)

details. Those modelers who normally re-detail their cockpits will find little to fault Revell about on this kit. (Purists may note that Revell's TF34 fan blades turn the wrong way, but few will care to do anything about it.)

Molding of parts is not as sharp as in the Tamiya kit, and some flash is present. However this is easily removed. Detailing is not as extensive, and this is most noticeable on the landing gear and ejection seat.

Also representing an early A-10A, the Revell model lacks the updates added to the actual aircraft. But these will have to be added to any 1/48th scale kit. The two releases are identical except for decals (covered below) and the color of the plastic used.

Stores include four Rockeyes, six Mavericks, a chaff/flare pod, and an ALQ-119. The ECM pod is mounted correctly this time, but should be longer.

Overall, this is a good kit for the money, and we recommend it.

DECAL SUMMARY

Note: It is impossible to completely review decals unless the reviewer has actually used the decals on a model to see how they fit. Additionally, markings on a given aircraft can be changed from time to time, so it is possible that the decals may be accurate for one point in time and not another. Therefore, this section is more of a listing of decals available than a review. Review comments are made only in regard to fit when we have actually used the decals or as to accuracy when the evidence clearly indicated an error.

KIT DECALS

1/144th SCALE KITS

LS Kit Number A-207: Contains markings for three aircraft, all of which are in the European 1 "Lizard" scheme.
- A-10A, 79-105, 47th TFS, 917th TFG, AFRES, BD tail code.
- A-10A, 78-612, 131st TFS, 104th TFG, Mass. ANG, MA tail code
- A-10A, 77-262, 81st TFW, WR tail code

LS Kit Number A-208: Contains markings for one aircraft, A-10A, 79-175, 23rd TFW, EL tail code, in the European 1 "Lizard" scheme with shark's mouth. This is the commander's aircraft.

100th SCALE KIT

Takara Kit Number 10: In addition to fictitious markings for the Royal Aslan Air Force, this kit contains markings for one A-10A, 75-281, 355th TFW, 333rd TFTS, in the MASK 10A gray scheme. The tail code is DM.

1/72nd SCALE KITS

Matchbox Kit Number PK-121: Contains markings for the first prototype, 711369, in the overall light gray scheme, and pre-production aircraft number 1, 731664, in an overall olive green scheme.

Monogram Kit Number 5405: Contains markings for an A-10A, 75-275, 355 TFW, DM tail code in the overall light gray scheme.

Monogram Kit Number 5430: Contains markings for an A-10A, 79-175, 23rd TFW, commander's aircraft. The aircraft is in the European 1 "Lizard" scheme with an EL tail code and shark's mouth.

Hasegawa/Minicraft Kit Number 1206: Provides markings for two aircraft.
- A-10A, 79-175, 23rd TFW, EL tail code, shark's mouth, in the European 1 "Lizard" paint scheme. This is the commander's aircraft.
- A-10A, 75-281, 333rd TFTS, 355th TFW, DM tail code, in the MASK 10A gray scheme.

Airfix/MPC Kit Number 1-4407: Contains markings for A-10A, 79-175, 23rd TFW, EL tail code, in the European 1 "Lizard" scheme with shark's mouth. This is the commander's aircraft.

1/48th SCALE KITS

ESCI Kit Number 4005: Contains markings for two A-10As, 75-260, and 75-261. Both aircraft are in the overall gray scheme with DM tail codes for the 355th TFW. As released earlier under the Scale Craft name in the U.S., A-10A, 75-254 from the same unit was provided instead. It was also in the light gray scheme with the DM tail code.

ESCI Kit Number 4070: Provides markings for A-10A, 79-175, 23rd TFW, EL tail code, in the European 1 "Lizard" scheme with shark's mouth. This is the commander's aircraft.

<u>Tamiya Kit Number MA-123:</u> Contains markings for four aircraft.
- First preproduction aircraft, 731664, in an overall olive green scheme
- Preproduction aircraft number 6, 73-1664, in AFSC markings and mottled two-tone gray scheme
- A-10A, 75-260, 333rd TFTS, 355th TTW, DM tail code, in the overall light gray scheme
- A-10A, 75-261, 333rd TFTS, 355th TFW, DM tail code, in the two-tone graded gray scheme

<u>Revell Kit Number 4503:</u> Contains markings for A-10A, 75-258, 57th TFTW, WA tail code in the J.A.W.S. "polka dot" desert scheme.

<u>Revell Kit Number 4516:</u> Contains markings for A-10A, 77-255, 81st TFW, WR tail code, in the European 1 "Lizard" scheme.

DECAL SHEETS

1/72nd SCALE SHEETS

<u>Microscale Sheet Number 72-285:</u> Provides markings for five aircraft, one of which is A-10A, 77-255, 81st TFW, WR tail code, in the European 1 "Lizard" scheme.

<u>Microscale Sheet Number 72-313:</u> Provides markings for twelve A-10s.
- Preproduction A-10 number 2, 73-1665, in a mottled gray scheme
- Preproduction A-10 number 3, 73-1666, in a dark ghost gray scheme
- Preproduction A-10 number 4, 73-1667, in the MASK 10A gray scheme
- Preproduction A-10 number 5, 73-1668, in a three-tone gray scheme and AFSC markings
- Preproduction A-10 number 6, 73-1669, in a three-tone gray scheme and AFSC markings
- A-10A, 75-259, with only USAF markings in an overall light gray scheme
- A-10A, 75-260, 355th TFW, DM tail code in an overall light gray scheme
- A-10A, 75-289, 355th TFW, DM tail code in the MASK 10A gray scheme
- A-10A, 75-264, 35th TFW, DM tail code in the MASK 10A gray scheme
- A-10A, 75-297, 57th TTW, WA tail code in the MASK 10A gray scheme
- A-10A, 75-262, 57th TTW, WA tail code in one of the J.A.W.S. "polka dot" schemes
- A-10A, 75-259, 57th TTW, WA tail code in another of the J.A.W.S. "polka dot" schemes

Notes: This sheet also provides extra numbers to make other serial number possibilities. However there are only enough general markings for four aircraft.

<u>Microscale Sheet Number 72-335:</u> Provides markings for nine A-10s.

- Preproduction A-10 number 5, 73-1668, in USAF markings and an overall light gray scheme
- A-10A, 79-180, 23rd TFW, EL tail code, European 1 scheme, commander's aircraft with shark's mouth
- A-10A, 78-675, 356th TFS, 354th TFW, MB tail code, European 1 scheme, commander's aircraft
- A-10A, 78-700, 66th FWS, 57th TTW, WA tail code, European 1 scheme
- A-10A, 78-607, 138th TFS, 174th TFG, New York ANG, "The Boys From Syracuse," European 1 scheme with NY tail
- code
- A-10A, 79-108, 118th TFS, 103rd TFG, Connecticut ANG, European 1 scheme with CT tail code
- A-10A, 78-637, 104th TFS, 175th TFG, Maryland ANG, European 1 scheme with MD tail code
- A-10A, 78-620, 131st TFS, 104th TFG, Massachusetts ANG, European 1 scheme with MA tail code
- A-10A, 79-136, 47th TFS, 917th TFG, AFRES, European 1 scheme with BD tail code

1/48th SCALE SHEETS

<u>Microscale Sheet Number 48-69:</u> Provides markings for the same twelve aircraft as sheet 72-313. The same notes also apply.

<u>Microscale Sheet Number 48-134:</u> Provides markings for five of the aircraft represented on sheet 72-335 as covered above. They are 731668, 78-700, 78-607, 79-108, and 78-637. The same markings and schemes are used.

<u>Microscale Sheet Number 48-135:</u> Provides markings for the other four aircraft included on sheet 72-335 as covered above. They are 78-675, 79-180, 78-620, and 79-136. It should be noted that on sheet 72-335, the diagonal tail bands on 78-675 are blue and red, while on this sheet they are blue, red, and black. One of the sheets is obviously in error. Both instruction sheets state that the aircraft is represented as of April 1981.

GLOSSARY

AAC Alaskan Air Command

AFFTC Air Force Flight Test Center (AFSC): based at Edwards AFB, CA.

AFRES Air Force Reserve.

AFSC Air Force Systems Command: orders, evaluates, and develops systems to the requirements of 'user commands.

ALE-40 The primary chaff/flare dispenser used by the A-10: mounted externally or (see pages 54 & 55) in the wing tips and wheel sponsons.

ALQ-119/131 ECM pods approved for the A-10: mounted on wing station 1 or 11.

ALS Ammunition Loading System

ANG Air National Guard

ASD Aeronautical Systems Division (of AFSC)

BDU-33 The standard lightweight practice bomb

BL-755 A British cluster weapon used successfully in the Falklands. Approved for use on the A-10 only in war-time emergency. The A-10 does not use the BL-755's electrical fusing system, and the mechanical fuse can cause premature opening and dispensing of submunitions.

BLU-52 Standard napalm canister

CAS Close Air Support

DT&E Development Test & Evaluation. Once a prototype is accepted, the DT&E part of a program determines if the aircraft works as expected. A-10 DT&E began on 19 March 1973, using prototype aircraft, though the first preproduction airframe was officially DT&E aircraft #1. This part of the program was run concurrent with IOT&E.

ECM Electronic Countermeasures

FOT&E Follow-on Operational Test and Evaluation. Determines tactics, techniques, and procedures for operational use; generates reliability and maintainability data and refines training requirements. A-10 FOT&E was run from 1975, through December 1977.

FS 595a The Federal Standard dealing with the color values of paints. Each approved color listed in this book is designated by a five-digit number from FS 595a. Copies of the color chips can be purchased from:
> GSA Specifications
> Room 6039
> 7th and D Streets SW
> Washington, DC 20407

FWS/FWW Fighter Weapons Squadron/Wing

GBU-8 2,000 pound (MK 84) TV-guided (or Electro-optical) bomb

GBU-10 2,000 pound (MK 84) laser-guided bomb

GBU-12 500 pound (MK 82) laser-guided bomb

HUD Head-up Display

INS Inertial Navigation System

IOT&E Initial Operational Test & Evaluation. Validates the utility, operational suitability, and effectiveness of the system; followed by production commitments. Run jointly by AFSC and TAC, Phase I began at Davis-Monthan on 19 March 1973. Phase II ran at Nellis from 19 March 1975, through 13 June 1975.

LAU-68 Podded rocket launcher; carries seven 2.75 inch folding-fin aerial rockets (FFAR)

LGB Laser-guided bomb

MAC Military Airlift Command: responsible for transport, air rescue, weather, and special operations aircraft (such as the AC-130). (MAC does not have any plans to turn the A-10 into a trash hauler!)

Maverick	The AGM-65 guided missile.
MER	Multiple ejector rack. Adapts a single wing station to hold and release six stores. The MER-10 was evaluated for the A-10, but not approved.
MK 20	Cluster bomb: the Rockeye
MK 36	Cluster bomb: the Destructor
MK 82	500 lb. bomb: used as low drag, general purpose (LDGP), Snakeye (SE or high drag, retarded-fall weapon), or as basis for a guided weapon.
MK 84	2,000 lb. bomb; used as low drag, general purpose (LDGP), or basis for guided weapon.
MTW	Maximum Takeoff Weight
MXU-648	Aircraft cargo pod: the luggage rack.
OT&E	Operational Test & Evaluation: the combination of IOT&E and FOT&E.
PACAF	Pacific Air Forces
RDT&E	Research, Development Test & Evaluation. Prior to production of a prototype, RDT&E attempts to determine if the necessary technology can be devised and applied, and if it is worth pursuing.
RFP	Request for Proposals. An invitation to the industry to submit approaches to filling a defined system requirement. The A-X RFP was let on 8 March 1970.
Rockeye	MK 20 Cluster bomb
SAC	Strategic Air Command. Responsible for strategic bomber and missile forces. (SAC has no plans to load cruise missiles on the A-10!)
SPO	System Program Office. The office at Aeronautical Systems Division (AFSC), responsible for coordinating development of a weapons system. The A-10 SPO (nee: "A-X SPO") was established 27 April 1970.
SUU-20	Training dispenser. Can drop BDU-33 practice bombs or launch 2.75 inch folding fin aerial rockets.
SUU—23	External 20mm Vulcan Gatling gun pod.
SUU—25	Flare dispenser. Can launch target markers or flares for night operations.
SUU-30	Bomblet dispenser. Used (depending on submunition) as the CBU-52, CBU-58, or CBU-71.
TAC	Tactical Air Command. The primary tactical combat command; along with AFSC, responsible for development of the A-10 for use by all combat commands.
TASS	Tactical Air Support Squadron. Standard designation for forward air control units.
TAWC	Tactical Air Warfare Center (TAC). Based at Eglin AFB, Florida.
TER	Triple ejector rack. Adapts a single wing station to hold and sequentially release three stores. The TER-9 is standard for the A-10.
TES	Test & Evaluation Squadron
TFS/TFG/TFW	Tactical Fighter Squadron/Group/Wing
TFTS	Tactical Fighter Training Squadron
TTW	Tactical Training Wing
TWS	Tactical Weapons Squadron
USAFE	US Air Forces, Europe
Warthog	Any of a genus (Phacochoerus) of African wild hogs with two pairs of rough warty excrescences on the face and large protruding tusks. For further information, see your local Air Force recruiter - BUT DON'T SIGN ANYTHING!